Britain's Best seaside escapes

Britain's Best
seaside
escapes

Annabelle Thorpe & Liz Bird

NEW HOLLAND

Dedication

Annabelle: For Lucy, Charlotte, Maddie, Amy, Ben and Sam and all our sunlit days by the sea.

Liz: To Matt, Eleanor and Bea and many more happy, fun-filled days on the beach.

This edition published in 2010
by New Holland Publishers (UK) Ltd
London • Cape Town • Sydney • Auckland

www.newhollandpublishers.com

Garfield House, 86–88 Edgware Road, London W2 2EA, United Kingdom

80 McKenzie Street, Cape Town 8001, South Africa

Unit 1, 66 Gibbes Street, Chatswood, NSW 2067, Australia

218 Lake Road, Northcote, Auckland, New Zealand

ISBN 978 1 84773 545 4

Publishing director: Rosemary Wilkinson
Project editor: Louise Coe
Editor: Clare Hubbard
Proofreader and indexer: Pamela Ellis
Designer: Isobel Gillan
Picture research: Isabel Kendrick, PPL Media
Cartography: William Smuts
Production: Marion Storz

Reproduction by Modern Age Repro House Ltd, Hong Kong
Printed and bound in Singapore by Tien Wah Press, Ltd

Page 1: View to Hughtown Harbour, St Mary's, Scilly Isles.
Pages 2–3: Sennen Cove, Cornwall, at dusk.
Above left: Eden Project, near St Austell, Cornwall.
Above centre: Fisherman's hut on Aldeburgh beach.
Above right: Puffin, Farne Islands, Northumberland

Main chapter opener images:
Pages 10–11: Calgary Bay, Isle of Mull.
Pages 34–35: Bamburgh Castle, Bamburgh.
Pages 62–63: Early morning at Blakeney Harbour.
Pages 80–81: The dramatic cliffs at Rhossili.
Pages 104–05: Durdle Door, Dorset.
Pages 134–35: Channel between Bryher and Tresco, Scilly Isles.

Contents

Introduction

The sea, the sea. As an island nation Britain is defined and dominated by the waters that surround it: the icy depths of the North Sea, the dramatic rollers of the Atlantic, the tranquil waters of the English Channel. Our coastal towns are part of our country's seafaring heritage; cobbled lanes once frequented by smugglers, ancient harbours where fishermen still land their catch and historic shipbuilding towns that reinvented themselves as elegant Victorian resorts.

Right: Idyllic stretch of beach at Studland, Dorset.

The British seaside evokes memories of idyllic childhood holidays spent building sandcastles, tucking into fish and chips and watching Punch and Judy shows on the pier; simple pleasures that have remained unchanged for decades. But this book isn't simply about the best places for a bucket-and-spade holiday. The beauty of the British coastline is in its diversity; from Northumberland's wild beaches and idyllic Scottish islands to the rugged Cornish coastline and the picturesque bays and unspoilt coves of Devon and Dorset.

Many seaside towns have undergone impressive regeneration over the past few years, with boutique hotels, sleek B&Bs and gastropubs offering quality, locally sourced dishes. All are ideal boltholes after a blustery day on the beach. For those on a budget well-equipped campsites dot the countryside, many offering teepees and wigwams for a really memorable stay.

The towns, villages, beaches and coastline we have chosen represent the best that Britain has to offer – and all have year-round experiences and activities that can create an unforgettable weekend away. From seal-spotting and bird-watching to coasteering and kiteboarding to fossil-hunting and fishing trips, there are infinite ways to discover Britain's coastline. But the simple pleasures of the seaside are still the best; set off on foot, walk the clifftops and the coastal paths, gaze out across the infinite skies and let the calm beauty of the sea simply wash over you.

Map of featured seaside escapes

Numbers correspond to those listed on the Contents page (see page 5) and opposite.

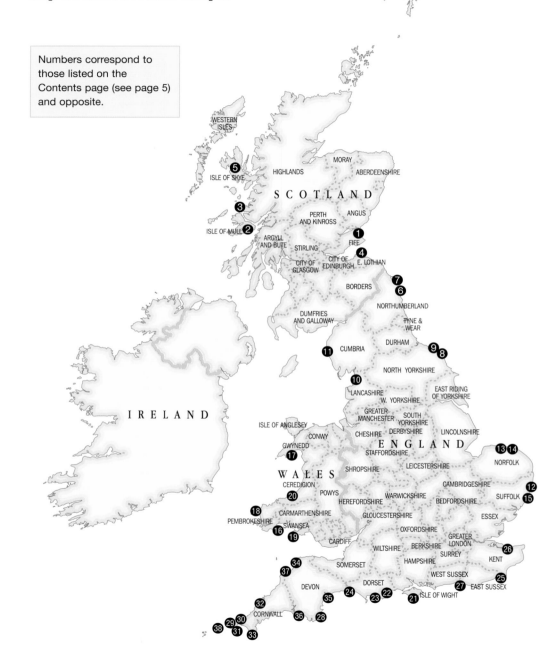

Where to go for...

NATURE
The best places for wildlife watching
2   Isle of Mull
3   Sanna Bay/Ardnamurchan
4   Yellowcraig
7   Bamburgh and the Farne Islands
10 Morecambe
11 St Bees
13 Holkham
14 Blakeney
15 Aldeburgh
16 Barafundle Bay
18 St David's
20 New Quay
22 Brownsea Island and Studland Bay
24 Lyme Regis and Charmouth
25 Rye

WALKING
The best places for scenic coastal walks
2   Isle of Mull
3   Sanna Bay/Ardnamurchan
4   Yellowcraig
5   Isle of Skye
6   Craster
7   Bamburgh and the Farne Islands
8   Robin Hood's Bay
9   Whitby
11 St Bees
13 Holkham
14 Blakeney
17 Llanbedrog
18 St David's
19 Rhossili
21 Isle of Wight

24 Lyme Regis and Charmouth
31 Wembury
32 Clovelly
33 Sennen Cove
34 St Ives
35 Porthcurno

GOOD FOOD
The best places for seafood and other local produce
2   Isle of Mull
5   Isle of Skye
6   Craster
9   Whitby
13 Holkham
14 Blakeney
15 Aldeburgh
20 New Quay
26 Whitstable
27 Brighton
34 St Ives
36 Newquay

FAMILY-FRIENDLY BEACHES
Good facilities and child-friendly activities
1   St Andrews
12 Southwold
13 Holkham
17 Llanbedrog
18 St David's (Whitesands)
22 Brownsea Island and Studland Bay
23 Lulworth Cove and Durdle Door
26 Whitstable
27 Brighton
28 Blackpool Sands
30 Woolacombe/Saunton Sands
33 Sennen Cove

34 St Ives (Porthmeor Beach)
36 Newquay

SPLENDID ISOLATION
The best places for long walks along unspoilt beaches
2   Isle of Mull
3   Sanna Bay/Ardnamurchan
4   Yellowcraig
5   Isle of Skye
7   Bamburgh and the Farne Islands
13 Holkham
16 Barafundle Bay
19 Rhossili
21 Isle of Wight
22 Brownsea Island and Studland Bay

ALL-ACTION HOLIDAYS
Seaside escapes offering action and adventure
16 Barafundle Bay
18 St David's (Whitesands)
19 Rhossili
30 Croyde/Woolacombe/Saunton Sands
33 Sennen Cove
36 Newquay

NIGHTLIFE
The best resorts for pubs and clubs
10 Morecambe
26 Whitstable
27 Brighton
34 St Ives
36 Newquay

SCOTLAND

St Andrews Fife

It took an Oscar-winning film to make St Andrews famous for something other than golf. The barefoot run along the sands in *Chariots of Fire* was filmed on West Sands beach.

RIGHT: The Doll's House restaurant in Church Square, St Andrews.

BELOW: West Sands beach is a 15-minute walk from St Andrews.

Today runners still pad along this 3-kilometre (2-mile) long strand on the northern coast of Fife, one of Scotland's few Blue Flag beaches. Its gently shelving sand and summer lifeguards make it popular with families, who flock to the town end. Its great expanse is a big draw for adrenalin-fuelled kiteboarders and sand yachters, who frequent the other end near the River Eden estuary.

If walking is more your thing, St Andrews forms part of the **Fife Coastal Path** (www.fifecoastalpath.co.uk), a 128.5-kilometre (80-mile) long walk from the Forth Road Bridge to the Tay Bridge, passing historic castles, nature reserves and pretty fishing villages. However, only hardy and experienced walkers should attempt the section between St Andrews and just north of Crail as there is rough and tidal terrain and the path can be difficult to follow.

Just behind the dune-backed **West Sands** beach are the links golf courses including the world-renowned Old Course (www.standrews. org.uk), the location for many Open Championships. When it's not hosting international competitions, mere mortals can play a round of golf

The ruins of St Andrew's Cathedral are a great place to wander.

RIGHT: Players have to cross the Swilcan Bridge on the 18th fairway on the Old Course.

here. Many golfers expect this to be a private members-only club but it's a public course; the only problem is getting a tee-off time. Either book months in advance or enter a ballot before 2 p.m. on the day before you wish to play. If all else fails at least you have ten other local courses to choose from.

Golf has been played at St Andrews since the 15th century and by 1457 James II banned it because it was interfering with his troops' archery practice. Find out more about the sport's history at the **British Golf Museum** (www.britishgolfmuseum.co.uk) with its interactive displays and memorabilia. It's located just a stone's throw from the Old Course on Bruce Embankment.

But this ancient compact town isn't all about golf; it has a charm of its own. The skyline is dominated by the majestic towers and spires of a ruined **castle** and **cathedral**. Climb the 12th-century cathedral's St Rule's Tower and you will be rewarded by breathtaking views of sea and sand stretching into the distance. The graveyard also has lots of monuments to philosophers, sailors and – naturally – golfers. But it's the castle that's most fascinating, with its complex of siege tunnels, one dug by the besiegers in 1547, the other more desperate and winding one dug by the besieged who heard them coming. There's also a bottle dungeon where you can peer through the narrow entrance and imagine how horrible it must have been to be imprisoned in its dark depths.

It's not all doom and gloom. This prosperous seaside town is a pleasant place to stroll around, with elegant, ivy-clad buildings, quadrangles and gardens. The town is home to an ancient university where wealthy English undergraduates rub shoulders with Scottish theology students. It also has a vibrant nightlife with plenty of bars and top-class restaurants.

One of the best places to eat is the simple and elegant **The Seafood Restaurant** (www.theseafoodrestaurant.com) housed in a 'glass box' overlooking West Sands. You'll feel like you're hovering over the beach as you tuck into local oysters and home-cured gravadlax and take in that stunning seascape.

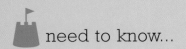

need to know...

ESSENTIAL · INFORMATION

SLEEP **The Old Course Hotel** is a five-star hotel with a spa overlooking the famous links courses and West Sands (01334 474371; www.oldcourse hotel.co.uk). **Shandon House**, 10 Murray Place, is a Victorian townhouse bed and breakfast in a central location. Locally smoked haddock or kippers and haggis for breakfast (01334 472412; www.shandonhouse.co.uk). **Cambo Estate**, just outside St Andrews, is a 485.5-hectare (1,200-acre) estate that offers self-catering cottages, serviced apartments and bed and breakfast (01333 450054; www.camboestate.com)

EAT **The Seafood Restaurant**, Bruce Embankment, is a stylish restaurant overlooking the beach that serves perfectly cooked fresh fish with a twist (01334 479475; www.theseafood restaurant.com). **PM's of St Andrews**, 1–3 Union Street, is a family-run fish and chip shop that also sells pizza, pasta and baked potatoes. Will deliver in the evening too (01334 476425; www.pmsof standrews.com). **The Doll's House Restaurant**, 3 Church Square, serves traditional Scottish and French cuisine with a contemporary twist (01334 477422; www.dolls-house.co.uk)

EXPLORE Discover St Andrews' less than saintly past on an 80-minute night-time tour of the city's landmarks with **Black Hart Tours** (0131 2259044; www.blackhart.uk.com). Take the family on a coastal scramble, where you traverse rocky cliffs with the help of a chain, just along the coast at Cellardyke, with **East Neuk Outdoors** (01333 311929; www.eastneukoutdoors.co.uk). It also offers mountain biking, canoeing and abseiling. Try off-road quad biking or laser clay pigeon shooting with **Fyfeoffroad**, Kinkell Farm, just outside St Andrews (01334 472003; www.fyfeoffroad.com)

TOURIST INFORMATION **St Andrews Tourist Information Centre**, 70 Market Street (01334 472021). **www.visit-standrews.co.uk**. **www.visitfife.com**

GETTING THERE **Nearest train station** is Leuchars (9 kilometres (5½ miles) away from St Andrews). **By road** the West Sands beach is accessed from the A91 Cupar to St Andrews road

GOOD FOR Activity holidays, couples, families, wildlife enthusiasts

Isle of Mull Argyll and Bute

You'll often see dolphins and sea otters swimming in the harbour at Tobermory, a pretty fishing port lined with brightly coloured houses on the Isle of Mull. The waters to the west of this Inner Hebridean island also provide some of the best whale-watching opportunities in Scotland.

RIGHT: *Looking towards Iona, a magical island where 48 of Scotland's kings are buried.*

Minke whales sometimes bob up next to the boat – as well as basking sharks, common and grey seals – on a six-hour long trip with **Sea Life Surveys** (www.sealifesurveys.co.uk), which operates from April to October.

One of the best ways to see Mull's abundant wildlife is by going on a **one-day safari** with Richard and Linda Atkinson (www.wildlifemull.co.uk). They know all the top spots to watch otters, red deer, kestrels and the rare white-tailed sea eagles with their amazing 2.5-metre (8-foot) wingspan; there are only 11 pairs on the whole island.

Mull has abundant birdlife such as kestrels, eagles and puffins.

Otters can also be seen around the old pier on the island's undisputed best beach, **Calgary Bay**. Situated on the north-west coast, it has silvery-white sand, clear water, craggy headlands filled with nesting seabirds and the windswept islands of Coll and Tiree shimmering in the distance.

Walk up the valley and you'll come to the remains of 20 houses of **Inivea**, once home to crofters who were forcibly removed, many of them ending up in Canada (Calgary in the Canadian province of Alberta is named after the beach). Now the only residents are sheep and highland cattle.

Mull is an excellent gateway to neighbouring islands, the most magical being tiny **Iona**, reached by ferry from Fionnphort on the south-west coast. St Colomba landed on Iona from Ireland in 563 before setting out to convert Scotland to Christianity. Stay overnight and you can walk up the hill for magnificent sea views or look around the ancient graveyard where 48 of Scotland's early kings, including Macbeth, are buried.

Take a boat trip to **Staffa** with **Turus Mara** (www.turusmara.com). The motion of the waves crashing into **Fingal's Cave**, formed from giant basalt columns, inspired Felix Mendelssohn's beautiful *Hebrides Overture*.

RIGHT: Colourful houses line the waterfront in Tobermory.

Many parents with young children probably know Mull better than they think; the capital **Tobermory** was the setting for the BBC's CBeebies children's show *Balamory*. In summer the place is overrun with excited children trying to spot PC Plum and other characters from the series. If you're in need of a stiff drink after all that rushing around, drop into **Tobermory Distillery** (www.tobermorymalt.com), which offers guided tours and produces two award-winning malt whiskies, 10-year-old Tobermory and Ledaig.

Kids will love the narrow gauge miniature steam train operated by the **Isle of Mull Railway** (www.mullrail.co.uk) that runs from **Craignure** – the destination for ferries from Oban on the mainland – to **Torosay Castle** (www.torosay.com), a rambling Victorian mansion set in a beautiful garden. Three kilometres (two miles) south-west is the magnificent **Duart Castle** (www.duartcastle.com), which stands proudly on a clifftop overlooking the Sound of Mull and is one of the oldest inhabited castles in Scotland.

The stunning landscape of Calgary Bay and the surrounding countryside.

Apart from scaling the island's highest peak – 966-metre (1,555-foot) high **Ben More** – for great views of the surrounding islands, Mull's best scenery can be found along its 483-kilometre (300-mile) long coast lined with precipitous cliffs, sea lochs and white sand beaches. One of the best and most challenging walks is the 6.5-kilometre (4-mile) trek to the **Carsaig Arches** at **Malcolm's Point**, with vertical drops and steep slopes along the way. Your efforts will be rewarded by the sight of natural rock arches, such as the towering 36-metre (118-foot) high 'keyhole'. And, like everywhere in Mull, you have a good chance of seeing some amazing wildlife, such as kittiwakes and eagles, along the way.

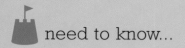

SLEEP Torosay Castle, Craignure, has two holiday cottages. **Gardener's Cottage**, which has two bedrooms, is situated within the formal gardens. **Shore Cottage**, a secluded one-bedroomed property, is about 800 metres (½ mile) from the castle and overlooks a sandy beach at Duart Bay (01680 812421; www.torosay.com). **Tobermory Campsite**, Newdale, is a quiet, family friendly site 2.5 kilometres (1½ miles) west of town (01688 302624; www.tobermory-campsite.co.uk). **Calgary Hotel**, Calgary, is a superb ten-room hotel with restaurant (see below) plus self-catering accommodation close to Calgary Bay (01688 400256; www.calgary.co.uk)

EAT The Dovecote Restaurant, Calgary Hotel, serves Tobermory smoked trout, island loin of pork and venison in a former dovecote with exposed beams and whitewashed walls (01688 400256; www.calgary.co.uk). **The Fisherman's Pier Fish and Chip Van** on Tobermory waterfront sells fresh prawns and scallops (April to December, every day except Sunday). **Café Fish**, The Pier, Tobermory, serves simply cooked fresh fish – some caught from the restaurant's own boat – plus home-made bread, locally sourced vegetables and has a great view from the terrace (01688 301253; www.thecafe fish.com)

EXPLORE Sea Life Surveys will take you on a two-hour Ecocruz, where you can listen to prawns 'chatting' on the seabed and dolphins through an underwater hydrophone and haul a lobster pot. It's ideal for young children who might get bored on a day-long whale-watching trip (01688 302916; www.sealifesurveys.co.uk). **Mull Magic** offers daily guided walking tours on the island, starting in Tobermory (01688 301213; www.mullmagic.com). **Brown's Tobermory**, 21 Main Street, Tobermory, will hire you a mountain bike so that you can head for the hills and explore the island (01688 302020; www.brownstobermory.co.uk)

TOURIST INFORMATION Craignure Visitor Information Centre, The Pier Head (08452 255121). **Tobermory Visitor Information Centre**, The Pier (08452 255121). **www.tobermory.co.uk**. **www.visitscottishheartlands.com**

GETTING THERE Nearest train station is Oban on the mainland. **By ferry** Caledonian MacBrayne operates ferries from Oban to Craignure, Kilchoan on the Ardnamurchan Peninsula to Tobermory and Lochaline to Fishnish on the east coast of Mull (08000 665000; www.calmac.co.uk)

GOOD FOR Activity holidays, couples, families, peace and quiet, wildlife enthusiasts

Sanna Bay/Ardnamurchan Highlands

The translation from Gaelic of Ardnamurchan means 'land of the great seas' and it's an apt description of this 129-square-hectare (50-square-mile) peninsula that stretches along the shores of Loch Sunart in Lochaber.

Mingary Castle was built in the 13th century.

RIGHT: Ardnamurchan is a stunningly beautiful place.

Isolated and with a wild, untamed beauty, the remote feel of this area is accentuated by the fact that access is by a single-track road that twists and turns for much of the peninsula's length. **Sanna** lies at the westernmost tip and is barely more than a clutch of crofters' cottages and some spectacular beaches. This is about as far away from a busy resort as you can get and although the journey can be long, the rewards are worthwhile.

There is just one small road that links the villages and hamlets and most of the major sights that are on any tourist's 'must-see list'. The first settlement is **Glenborrodale** and just to the west of the hamlet is the **Ardnamurchan Natural History Centre** (www.ardnamurchannatural historycentre.co.uk), which has an excellent photographic exhibition of local wildlife and interactive exhibits.

A short distance to the east of the village is the **Royal Society for the Protection of Birds's nature reserve** (www.rspb.org.uk), where it's possible to see otters and seals, with eagles swooping in the skies above.

A little further on is the sweeping bay of **Camus nan Geall**, where a prehistoric standing stone helps create a mystical feel.

The village of **Kilchoan**, the most westerly village on mainland Britain, is the main settlement on the peninsula and it makes an ideal base; the ancient ruins of **Mingary Castle** are nearby, there are ferry links to the **Isle of Mull** (see page 16) and it is a short drive from both Sanna Bay and the lighthouse at Ardnamurchan Point. A day trip across to the pretty town of **Tobermory**, with its prettily painted houses, may be a favourite choice with young children as it was the location for the popular children's series *Balamory*.

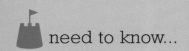

need to know...

ESSENTIAL · INFORMATION

SLEEP **Tir Na Og**, Sanna Bay, is a traditional crofters' cottage that sleeps six, just two minutes' walk over the dunes to the beach (01972 510262; www.sannabaycottage.co.uk). **Sonachan Hotel**, Kilchoan, is the UK's most westerly hotel, set on a working farm with comfortable bedrooms as well as bunkhouse accommodation (01972 510211; www.sannabay.com). **Ardshealach Lodge**, Acharacle, offers bed and breakfast and a self-catering cottage in a stunning location on the banks of Loch Sheil (01967 431399; www.ardshealach-lodge.co.uk; to book cottage send email through website)

EAT **Kilchoan House Hotel**, Kilchoan, is also the village pub and serves up hearty meals of locally caught fish in its cosy bar (01972 510 200; www.kilchoanhousehotel.co.uk). **Glen Uig Inn**, Lochailort, serves local game and seafood, just a step away from the beach (01687 470219; www.glenuig.com). **Ardnamurchan Natural History Centre**,

Glenmore, Acharacle, is a nice stop for tea and cake; also offers light lunches made with local produce (01972 500209; www.ardnamurchan naturalhistorycentre.co.uk)

EXPLORE **Rockhopper Sea Kayaking** offers guided kayaking trips in the area (07739 837344; www.rockhopperscotland.co.uk). **Caledonian MacBrayne** runs ferries from Kilchoan to Tobermory on the Isle of Mull (08000 665000; www.calmac.co.uk)

TOURIST INFORMATION
www.ardnamurchan.com

GETTING THERE **Nearest train station** is Fort William (92.5 kilometres (57½ miles) away from Sanna). **By road** the only route on to the Ardnamurchan Peninsula is a single-track road, the B8007, accessible from the A861

GOOD FOR Couples, walkers, wildlife enthusiasts

From Kilchoan, it's a short drive to Sanna. En route you will pass over the centre of a crater of a long-extinct volcano and some of the most arresting scenery in the whole of Scotland. On a sunny day **Sanna Bay** is quite simply breathtaking: white-shell sand and turquoise water with dramatic views across to the islands of **Eigg**, **Muck** and **Canna** (along with Rum, these are the main islands known as the Small Isles). To the south of the bay lies **Ardnamurchan Point**, home to the Ardnamurchan lighthouse that marks mainland Britain's most westerly point.

The best way to experience the pensinula is on the water and there is great kayaking and sailing on offer, in the sound of **Arisaig** to the north

of the peninsula or **Loch Sunart** to the south. Designated a Special Area of Conservation, the loch is home to a rich array of wildlife; otters, seals and red deer can all be spotted. Even just strolling on the beach at Sanna offers the chance to see whales and dolphins and the Ardnamurchan lighthouse runs a whale- and dolphin-recording project, with excellent viewing facilities.

The peninsula is a wild and isolated place but the bright lights of **Fort William** are an easy drive away, offering a good selection of shops and restaurants, and provide a dramatic contrast to the stunning natural beauty of Ardnamurchan.

Unspoilt Sanna Bay,
Ardnamurchan Peninsula.

Yellowcraig East Lothian

Rolling sand dunes, unspoilt landscapes and a feeling of escape make Yellowcraig Beach a real find. Tucked away on the coast of East Lothian, the beach looks across to the tiny island of Fidra, which was believed to have provided the inspiration for Robert Louis Stevenson's classic novel *Treasure Island*.

Looking out from Yellowcraig to Fidra.

Protected from the winds that bluster along many of Scotland's beaches, **Yellowcraig** is perfect for a family day out, with a *Treasure Island*-themed play park and plenty of space for kite flying or football.

This corner of the Scottish coast is steeped in history; there are dramatic castles to explore and atmospheric villages to discover just a short drive from Yellowcraig. The nearby town of **North Berwick**, with its bustling harbour, supplies a good range of places to stay and eat and the pretty villages of Gullane and Dirleton are also close by. **Tantallon Castle** (www.historic-scotland.gov.uk), a short drive from North Berwick, is dramatically located on a promontory overlooking the sea and dates back to the 14th century.

    Dirleton is dominated by an equally atmospheric 13th-century castle (www.historic-scotland.gov.uk) that overlooks the village green. It is an impressive ruin with endless nooks and crannies for kids to crawl into

View of Tantallon Castle.

and scramble over. The castle is most famous for its beautiful gardens, with long elegant lawns and, according to *Guinness World Records*, the longest herbaceous border in the world. **Gullane** is one of the prettiest villages in the area, with its own stunning beach – **Gullane Bents**.

There is an enjoyable 9.5-kilometre (6-mile walk) from Dirleton to Gullane, which takes in Yellowcraig Beach and the world-famous **Muirfield Golf Course** (www.muirfield.org.uk), which has hosted the Open Championship. Muirfield is just one of nineteen courses in the area, all with affordable green fees and friendly clubhouses. Book a round at **Musselburgh Links** (www.musselburgholdlinks.co.uk) and you'll be playing on the oldest course in the world and you can hire hickory clubs to experience the game as it used to be.

The wildlife that flocks to the coast around Yellowcraig is awe-inspiring. The **Scottish Seabird Centre** (www.seabird.org), situated on The Harbour, North Berwick, is home to puffins and guillemots, razorbills and the largest single gannet colony in the world. Boat trips organized by the centre run out to **Bass Rock**, a 96-metre (315-foot) high slab of rock that becomes home to over 100,000 gannets each summer.

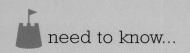

need to know...

SLEEP **The Open Arms**, Main Street, Dirleton, sits opposite the 13th-century castle and offers comfortable rooms and a warm welcome (01620 850241; www.openarmshotel.com). **The Glebe House**, Law Road, North Berwick, is a luxurious bed and breakfast in a 13th-century manse (01620 892608; www.glebehouse-nb.co.uk). **Tantallon Caravan & Camping Park**, North Berwick, has great wooden wigwams that are ideal for families (01620 893348; www.meadowhead.co.uk)

EAT **Bass Rock Bistro**, 37–39 Quality Street, North Berwick, offers fantastic locally caught lobster and fish (01620 890875; www.bassrock bistro.co.uk). **Village Coffee House**, 10 Rosebery Place, Gullane, has delicious home-made cakes (01620 842509). **La Potinière**, Main Street, Gullane, serves beautifully presented, locally sourced meat and fish and is renowned as one of the best restaurants in the area (01620 843214; www.la-potiniere.co.uk)

EXPLORE **Scottish Seabird Centre** runs a one-hour round trip seabird seafari wildlife-watching boat trip from North Berwick Harbour (01620 890202; www.seabird.org/boat-trips.asp). **Cycle** and **walking** routes can be downloaded (www.visit eastlothian.org)

TOURIST INFORMATION **North Berwick Tourist Information Centre**, 1 Quality Street (01620 892197). **www.visiteastlothian.org**

GETTING THERE **Nearest train station** is North Berwick (5.5 kilometres (3½ miles) from Yellowcraig). **By road** leave the A198 and follow the signs to Dirleton, from where the beach is signposted

GOOD FOR Activity holidays families, wildlife enthusiasts

There's plenty of life under the water as well as above it. Dolphins, porpoises and even whales can all be seen on boat trips and from October to December boats run to the **Isle of May Nature Reserve** to see dozens of fluffy, newborn seal pups.

On rainy days, the **National Museum of Flight** (www.nms.ac.uk) is a fantastic day out. It is located on East Fortune Airfield, which is one of the most famous sites in aviation history; it was the take-off point for the first aircraft to fly east–west across the Atlantic in 1919.

When the sun comes out again it's worth the stiff climb up **North Berwick Law**, a volcanic crag that tops 182 metres (600 feet) and gives stunning views across this beautiful stretch of coastline.

LEFT: Bass Rock holds approximately 10 per cent of the world's population of North Atlantic gannets.

Isle of Skye Highlands

There is something magical about the Isle of Skye. Joined to the mainland by a road bridge it nonetheless retains a unique island feel. It is a dramatic land of towering peaks, craggy cliffs and lush valleys with tranquil villages hidden in between.

RIGHT: The dramatic waterfall at Kilt Rock, on the east coast of the Trotternish Peninsula.

Skye is a place for exploring; from the white coral beaches and plummeting cliffs in the north to the **Sleat Peninsula** in the south, unexpectedly dotted with palm trees and plantations.

The island's capital, **Portree**, makes an ideal base as it is equidistant between the spectacular walking routes that criss-cross the island's north-east **Trotternish Peninsula** and the pretty villages, such as **Advasar**, on the east coast. The town is clustered around the harbour, where fishing boats and pleasure craft glide in and out, overlooked by a row of pretty pastel-coloured cottages on one side and traditional whitewashed houses on the other. The main shopping streets radiate out from **Somerled Square**. A browse in the craft shops and galleries on **Wentworth Street** is an ideal way to adjust to the gentle pace of life on the island. Portree is also home to **Aros** (www.aros.co.uk), a heritage centre in which you could while away an afternoon on a rainy day.

Skye has a thriving arts scene and many painters and craftspeople have made the island their home: drop in on **Edinbane Pottery** (www.edinbane-pottery.co.uk) in Edinbane for beautiful ceramics and seascapes; atmospheric watercolours from the **Aird Old Church Gallery** (www.skyewatercolours.co.uk) on the Sleat Peninsula; and beautiful Celtic jewellery from **Skye Jewellery** (www.skye-jewellery.co.uk) in the town of Broadford.

It's also a walkers' paradise (www.walkhighlands.co.uk), with challenging routes such as the 16-kilometre (10-mile) **Trotternish Ridge Walk** that offers astonishing views from the lofty path. There are gentler family walks such as the **Fairy Glen** near Uig, where kids can happily scramble over the rocks and gullies.

The Quiraing is one of the most spectacular features on the Trotternish Ridge Walk.

Days on Skye are not for lazing on the beach but for having unforgettable adventures – on foot or horseback, by boat or bicycle. The waters around the island are filled with sealife. Daily boat trips head out to see seals, otters, dolphins and whales including the **Seaprobe Atlantis** (www.seaprobeatlantis.com), Scotland's only semi-submersible glass-bottomed boat. The rivers also teem with fish, making it an ideal destination for anglers, with companies such as **Skye Ghillie Fishing** (www.skyeghillieflyfishing.co.uk) offering fishing days that can be combined with guided walks. Most boat trips and activities operate from April to October.

What makes Skye unique is that it combines a wild, remote feel with hotels and restaurants that offer real luxury and award-winning food. Mussels and lobster are lifted straight from the sea to your plate, rich cheeses are made in the village of **Achmore** and the traditional Scottish dessert of cranachan – oatmeal and cream – comes laced with local honey and Talisker whisky. It's impossible to visit Skye without a drop or two of Talisker and the distillery in **Carbost** (www.taliskerwhisky.com) is a good place to learn a little about Scotland's most famous export. But the best time for a whisky is when you're relaxing in front of the fire in a cosy pub, after an afternoon walking through some of the most dramatically beautiful landscapes that Scotland has to offer.

RIGHT: Portree harbour is in a beautiful setting, surrounded by high ground and cliffs.

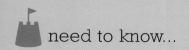

SLEEP **Ullinish Country Lodge**, Struan, is an award-winning restaurant with rooms that specializes in seafood; foodies should splurge on a night here (01470 572214; www.theisleofskye. co.uk). **Tigh an Dochais**, 14 Harrapool, offers a 21st-century twist on the traditional bed and breakfast. Designed by award-winning architects with floor to ceiling windows offering stunning views over Broadford Bay (01471 820022; www. skyebedbreakfast.co.uk). **Staffin Campsite**, Staffin, is surrounded by rugged scenery and has good facilities. There is also a two-bedroom self-catering cottage (01470 562213; www.staffin campsite.co.uk)

EAT **The Three Chimneys**, Colbost, is where serious gourmets should head for. This world-famous restaurant is housed in a former crofters' cottage and serves up beautifully presented dishes. There is also accommodation available in six junior suites in **The House Over-By**, just a few steps across the courtyard from the restaurant (01470 511258; www.threechimneys.co.uk). **Stein Inn**, Waternish, offers local seafood, meats and Scottish specialities (try the haggis toastie) (01470 592362; www.stein-inn.co.uk). **Café Arriba**, Quay Brae, Portree, serves great home-made cakes and vegetarian dishes (01478 611830; www.cafearriba. co.uk)

EXPLORE **The Isle of Skye Trekking Centre**, Suladale, offers you the chance to explore the area on horseback (01470 582419; www.theisleofskye trekkingcentre.co.uk). **Guiding on Skye** will take you on a trek through the Cullin Mountains with guide George Yeomans (01478 650380; www. guidingonskye.co.uk)

TOURIST INFORMATION **Portree Tourist Information Centre**, Bayfield House (01478 612137). **www.skye.co.uk**

GETTING THERE **Nearest train stations** are Mallaig on the mainland, from where the ferry goes to Armadale on Skye; or Kyle of Lochalsh, which is at the mainland edge of the Skye Bridge. **By road** the Skye Bridge, part of the A87, connects mainland Highland to the Isle of Skye

GOOD FOR Couples, wildlife enthusiasts

Craster Northumberland

At the heart of Northumberland's spectacular Heritage Coast, the village of Craster feels as if it belongs to another era. It was named after the Craster family, who have lived in the village for almost a millennium.

RIGHT: The dramatic ruins of Dunstanburgh Castle.

In the 19th century it was a thriving fishing village, with smokehouses and fishing yards that exported barrels of mackerel and herring as far afield as Russia and Germany. Nowadays just one smokehouse remains. The village has a quaint feel, with cottages overlooking the harbour and a sleepy high street.

Craster makes a great base for exploring this impressive stretch of coastline. The area boasts vast ruined castles, great sweeps of sandy beach, rocky outcrops and sand dunes, making it perfect for family days by the sea. The **Northumberland Coastal Path** runs through Craster, with a dramatic 16-kilometre (10-mile) walk to the long golden sands at **Embleton Bay**. There's also a shorter circular walk, but both take in the dramatic windswept ruins of **Dunstanburgh Castle**, one of the largest and grandest fortifications in northern England, that dates back to the 14th century. Owned by the National Trust (www.nationaltrust.org.uk), it offers fantastic views and even on a sunny day has a brooding, atmospheric feel. The ruins watch over a headland that is famous for its spectacular birdlife, including kittiwakes and razorbills and large numbers of migrating passerines.

Craster is famous for its smoked kippers.

It's impossible to spend time in this part of the country without a visit to **Alnwick Castle** (www.alnwickcastle.com). This stunning medieval castle – second only to Windsor Castle in terms of size – will seem eerily familiar after countless appearances in TV series such as *Blackadder* and in films, including the first two Harry Potter movies and *Elizabeth*.

Alnwick is also home to the **Alnwick Garden** (www.alnwickgarden.com), started in the late 1990s by the Duchess of Northumberland and home to the country's largest collection of European plants: swathes of roses, beds of delphiniums, bulbs and blossom in the spring and glorious

colours in the autumn. Kids will love it as it has fountains to play in, rope bridges to climb and mini tractors to drive.

A few miles on from Alnwick lies the town of **Rothbury**, which is a gateway to the stunning landscapes of the **Northumberland National Park** (www.northumberlandnationalpark.org.uk). The park has extensive walking, cycling and horse-riding routes, with terrain that changes from open moorland to lush green valleys, and is studded with picturesque villages such as **Elsdon** and **Alwinton**.

But the unique draw in this part of the country is the coastline and its heady combination of stunning natural scenery and dramatic history. For the perfect seaside day out, head to **Low Newton by the Sea**, a sleepy fishing village now owned by the National Trust. The village comprises a set of pretty cream cottages around a village green that looks out across the beach of **Newton Haven**. It's also home to the most northerly microbrewery in the UK at the **Ship Inn** (www.shipinn newton.co.uk). Try a half of Sand Castles at Dawn or Ship Hot Ale, along with drinking in the beautiful views.

RIGHT: Cheviot Hills, Northumberland National Park.

BELOW: Walk along the Northumberland Coastal Path.

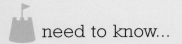

need to know...

ESSENTIAL • INFORMATION •

SLEEP Fisherman's Cottage is one of a handful of self-catering houses in the heart of Craster, sleeping up to six. Book through Northumberland Cottages (01665 589434; www.northumberland cottages.com). **Proctors Stead** is a camping and caravan site that is 1.5 kilometres (1 mile) from the sea with excellent facilities (01665 576613; www.proctorsstead.co.uk). **The Old Rectory**, Howick, is an elegant bed and breakfast, filled with period touches (01665 577590; www.oldrectory howick.co.uk)

EAT L. Robson & Sons, 9 Haven Hill, has been producing kippers for almost 100 years and has supplied them to the royal family; you must buy some and cook them for your breakfast (01665 576223; www. kipper.co.uk). **The Cottage Inn**, Dunstan Village, does excellent Sunday roasts and serves locally sourced meats and seafood (01665 576658; www.cottageinnhotel.co.uk). **The Red**

Lion, 22 Northumberland Street, Alnmouth, is an 18th-century coaching inn with an open fire, regional ales and steaks and sausages supplied from local farms (01665 830584; www.redlion alnmouth.com)

EXPLORE Shepherds Walks offer guided walks around the area (01830 540453; www.shepherds walks.co.uk)

TOURIST INFORMATION
www.visitnorthumberland.com

GETTING THERE Nearest train station is Alnmouth (13.5 kilometres (8.5 miles) from Craster). **By road** Craster is signposted from the B1339, which connects with the A1068

GOOD FOR Couples, families, walkers, wildlife enthusiasts

Bamburgh and the Farne Islands
Northumberland

The combination of dramatic castles and unspoilt beaches makes the Northumberland coast one of the most stunning – and yet least visited – parts of the UK. Bamburgh is dominated by the vast sandstone castle that stands on a massive outcrop looking out to the Farne Islands.

RIGHT: Birds nesting on the Farne Islands.

BELOW: The vast beach at Bamburgh, over-looked by the castle.

Overlooking a wide sweep of sandy beach, the castle dates back to the 11th century, a time when Northumberland was one of the most powerful regions in Britain.

The beach itself is breathtaking, miles of uninterrupted white sand, with submerged sandbars that make it great for surfing. Backed by sand dunes, it's the perfect spot in summer, while in winter it's moodily

romantic, with blustery winds and roaring waves hurtling towards the imposing castle. This is not a beach where you will ever have a problem finding space; even in August there's plenty of room for everyone.

The village is just a short walk from the beach and has some good accommodation options and an agreeably sleepy atmosphere. On a rainy day, it's worth visiting the **Grace Darling Museum** (www.rnli. org.uk) on Radcliffe Road, named after the Bamburgh woman who became a local heroine in the 1830s when she rowed a mile in stormy seas to rescue the survivors of a shipwreck. The museum has workshops and interactive exhibits about the rescue.

There are some good short walks from the village. It's just 5 kilometres (3 miles) along the coast to the historic village of **Seahouses**, and there is a regular bus service between the two if you only want to walk in one

direction. One of the best circular walks takes in the stunning beach at **Budle Bay**, and is a pleasant 6.5-kilometre (4-mile) stroll.

There are almost 30 islands in the Farne archipelago; some are only visible at low tide but all are home to an impressive array of wildlife. Daily boat trips run to the biggest island, Inner Farne. Now a bird sanctuary, it becomes home to thousands of puffins, razorbills, guillemots and cormorants during the summer, who come to the islands to nest. There are also several seal colonies dotted throughout the islands, with an estimated 4,000 seals in the area and around 1,000 new seal pups born every autumn.

You can't visit this part of the world without spending the day on **Lindisfarne**. This tidal island is cut off from the mainland by the tides twice a day and is most famous for its ruined eighth-century monastery, where the *Lindisfarne Gospels* – an illuminated manuscript – was written. The island is accessible by car but it is essential to be aware of the tide time otherwise an unplanned overnight stay can become a necessity! Besides the ruins of the priory there is a dramatic hilltop castle and much of the island is a nature reserve given over to the impressive numbers of wintering bird populations. The island also has stretches of wild and unspoilt beach backed by soft dunes that are often surprisingly quiet.

ABOVE: Puffins make their home on Inner Farne.

RIGHT: The isolated splendour of Lindisfarne's castle.

BELOW: Lindisfarne's unique beach huts.

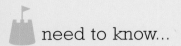

need to know...

ESSENTIAL • INFORMATION

SLEEP **Budle Hall**, situated just west of Bamburgh, is a listed Georgian house that offers very upmarket bed and breakfast accommodation. There are dinner parties in the evening and beautiful gardens (01668 214297; www.budle hall.com). **Springhill Farm**, Seahouses, has a campsite and self-catering accommodation in converted barns, with a well-stocked shop on site (01665 721820; www.springhill-farm.co.uk). **The Bamburgh Castle Inn**, Seahouses, has a great location on the quayside, smart bedrooms and an excellent restaurant (01665 720283; www. bamburghcastlehotel.co.uk)

EAT **The Lord Crewe** offers two dining options – excellent pub grub in Forsters Bar and more formal dishes in the Olive Tree restaurant; accommodation also available (01668 214243; www.lordcrewe. co.uk). **The Copper Kettle Tea Rooms**, 21 Front Street, is perfect for post-walk tea and cake. Everything is home-made, from quiches to carrot cake (01668 214315; www.copperkettle

tearooms.com). **Blacketts of Bamburgh**, 2 Lucker Road, is an award-winning wine bar and bistro that serves up locally caught fish, hefty home-made puds and has an excellent selection of off-sale wines (01668 214714)

EXPLORE **Glad Tidings Farne Island Boat Trips**, kiosk on the harbour (during main holiday season) at Seahouses, runs daily sailings from April–October, sailings by arrangement from November–March (01665 720308; www.farne-islands.com)

TOURIST INFORMATION
www.bamburgh.org.uk
www.visitnorthumberland.com

GETTING THERE **Nearest train station** is Berwick-upon-Tweed (34 kilometres (21 miles) from Bamburgh). **By road** take the B1341 to Bamburgh

GOOD FOR Couples, families, nature lovers, wildlife enthusiasts

Robin Hood's Bay North Yorkshire

Coastal villages don't come much more picturesque than this Yorkshire gem with its cobbled lanes and old fishermen's cottages tumbling down a precipitous slope to the North Sea.

RIGHT: At low tide the village beach is great for fossil hunting.

At low tide the rocky beach becomes surprisingly sandy and you'll often see people scouring the shore and rock pools, which are rich hunting grounds for fossils. The beaches and sheer cliffs along this rugged coast are full of reptilian and dinosaur fossils and footprints from the Jurassic and Cretaceous eras.

You can learn more about the geology of the area at the tiny **Robin Hood's Bay Museum** (http://museum.rhbay.co.uk/) on Fisherhead on the south side of the village, which has a fun model of a smuggler's house showing how contraband was once hidden.

One of the museum's most interesting exhibits tells of the numerous shipwrecks and historic rescues from this storm-battered coast. The story of the brig *Visitor* in 1881 has to be the most incredible. The storm was so great that the lifeboat couldn't be launched from Robin Hood's Bay so Whitby's lifeboat was dragged overland in a blizzard, 9.5 kilometres (6 miles) across the moors, to 'Bay'. Over 200 men dug through snowdrifts 2 metres (7 feet) high before the boat was taken down the steep hill to the sea. All of the crew were rescued and a plaque was laid in the town in 1981 to commemorate the men's steely determination. Less fortunate mariners are buried in the graveyard of St Stephen's Church, which lies high above the village on the road to Whitby.

Characterful fishermen's cottages line the steep, cobbled lanes.

If you're driving to Robin Hood's Bay the upper village is the place to leave your car. Walk past 19th-century ship captains' villas to **Old Bay** via a maze of narrow lanes and passages dotted with tea rooms, pubs, craft shops and artists' studios. One of the nicest places to have coffee and cake is the **Swell Café** (www.swell.org.uk), with its terrace overlooking the beach. It also has a unique sideline; a gorgeous old cinema with 1820s chapel pews as seating.

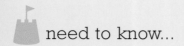

SLEEP **Old Coastguard Station** – within the station is a one-bed apartment on the second floor owned by National Trust Cottages (0844 8002070; www.nationaltrustcottages.co.uk). **Bramblewick**, The Dock, Old Village, housed in the village's former bakery predating 1650, is a restaurant with three en suite double rooms (01947 880339; www.bramblewick.org). **Middlewood Farm**, Middlewood Lane, Fylingthorpe, has space for tents, motorhomes and touring caravans at its campsite that is only a 10-minute walk from Robin Hood's Bay (01947 880414; www.middlewood farm.com)

EAT **Maryondale Fisheries**, Albion Road, does great fish and chips and you can eat in the café, which has open coal fires, oak floors and stone walls (01947 880426). **The Wayfarer Bistro**, Station Road, serves fresh fish and local beef and lamb; also offers accommodation (01947 880240; www.wayfarerbistro.co.uk). **The Old Bakery Tea Rooms**, Chapel Street, serves freshly baked cakes and scones, and snacks and sandwiches made using local produce (01947 880709)

EXPLORE **North East Yorkshire Geology Trust**, 5 Station Workshops, Station Road, leads guided walks in the Bay to look for fossils and learn more about the area's geology (01947 881000; www. neyorksgeologytrust.com). **Farsyde Riding Centre** caters for riders of all abilities; you can go pony trekking along the rail path, beach, fields and moorland for one to three hours (01947 880249; www.farsydefarmcottages.co.uk). **Trailways**, located on the Coastal Cycle Railtrail between Whitby and Robin Hood's Bay, hires out bikes; go cycling along the 128.5-kilometre (80-mile) Moor to Sea route, taking in Dalby and Langdale forests (01947 820207; www.trailways.info)

TOURIST INFORMATION **www.robin-hoods-bay.co.uk. www.northyorkmoors.org.uk. www.discoveryorkshirecoast.com**

GETTING THERE **Nearest train station** is Whitby (8 kilometres (5 miles) from Robin Hood's Bay). **By road** Robin Hood's Bay is north of Scarborough off the A171

GOOD FOR Activity holidays, couples, families, walkers, wildlife enthusiasts

The village also boasts some atmospheric pubs such as **The Laurel Inn** (01947 880400) on New Road, with its old brickwork, open fire, real ale and freshly made stone baps and soup served in winter; just what you need when it's blowing a gale.

The **Old Coastguard Station**, at the bottom of the bank, next to the slipway, is an interesting place to learn more about the Bay and the seashore and is used as an information centre for the **North York Moors National Park** (www.northyorkmoors.org.uk).

If you can tear yourself away from this photogenic village there are some excellent walks along the magnificent cliffs to the south, with tremendous views down to the 'scars' or swirling rock pavements that lie exposed at low tide. Have a cup of tea at the **Raven Hall Hotel** (www.ravenhall.co.uk) at **Ravenscar**, the Victorian spa town that never was due to the building company folding, and make your way back to the Bay along the disused Whitby to Scarborough railway line, an inland path sheltered from the bracing winds along the cliffs. It's also a popular cycle route.

The Bay is also renowned as the finishing point of Alfred Wainwright's 309-kilometre (192-mile) **Coast to Coast Walk** from St Bees in Cumbria (see page 58). When the walkers reach Robin Hood's Bay they celebrate by dipping their tired feet in the icy waters of the North Sea.

Another spectacular sunrise on Robin Hood's Bay.

LEFT: Fishing boats on the beach at 'Bay'.

Whitby North Yorkshire

This traditional North Yorkshire resort, with its strong seafaring history, windswept ruined abbey, pretty cobbled streets and great seafood, has wide-ranging appeal.

Even goths love **Whitby**. They adore the 13th-century **abbey** that dominates the skyline above the East Cliff, which inspired Victorian novelist Bram Stoker to use it as the setting for Count Dracula's dramatic landfall. Fans can visit the walk-through **Dracula Experience** (www.dracula experience.co.uk) on Marine Parade, but be warned, it's not for the faint-hearted. At the bottom of the abbey is the **Whitby Jet Heritage Centre** (www.whitbyjet.net/), a sign of the 19th-century penchant for mourning accessories. The fossilized wood was mined from local sea cliffs and is now popular with goths, who flock here for regular festivals.

The abbey is reached by 199 steps (you have to count them as you go up), which pass another of the town's gems, **St Mary's Church**, with its box pews and triple-decker pulpit with ear trumpets that once connected the hard of hearing to the sermon via a vast network of pipes.

Whitby is a town of two halves on either side of the River Esk, linked by a busy swing bridge. On the older east side is the abbey and its quaint cobbled streets are now home to lots of chic shops, atmospheric inns and tea rooms. On the other side are the beach, fish market and amusement arcades.

The town's biggest claim to fame is its association with Captain Cook, who served his apprenticeship as a seaman between 1747 and 1755 at a house in Grape Lane, now the **Captain Cook Memorial Museum** (www.cookmuseum whitby.co.uk). All of the ships used on his three world voyages were built on the banks of the River Esk just below the house. A bronze statue of Whitby's most famous explorer – often with a seagull perched on his head – stands proudly on the West Cliff next to the Whalebone Arch, commemorating the town's whaling past.

Whitby's famous kippers are just one of the town's seafood delights.

Today Whitby's main business is tourism, with the golden sands of **West Cliff beach** pulling in the crowds. There are rock pools, donkey rides and amusement arcades. Walk along the shore to **Sandsend** and you can drink Yorkshire tea and eat delicious home-made cake at the aptly named **Wit's End Café** (www.witsendcafe.co.uk). Nearby is the bustling quayside fish market, only a stone's throw away from the town's numerous fish and chip shops, the most famous being the **Magpie Café** (www.magpiecafe.co.uk) on Pier Road where people queue along the street to buy its crisp battered fish. If you like your fish a bit more imaginatively cooked the Egon Ronay-rated **Green's of Whitby** (www.greensofwhitby.com) is the place to go. Most mornings you can see the restaurant's Rob Green selecting fresh fish from the quayside, making its way on to the menu as creamy crab bisque or queen scallops grilled in the shell with parmesan, pesto and ham.

The hinterland of Whitby is dominated by a vast area of high moorland, which becomes a sea of purple heather in summer and forms part of the northern half of the **North York Moors National Park** (www.northyorkmoors.org.uk). Sliced through by lush dales and tidy villages, it makes a nice contrast to the hustle and bustle of Whitby. One of the nicest ways to see it is on a steam train to **Pickering** with North York Moors Railway (www.nymr.co.uk), which stops at **Goathland**, also known as Aidensfield in the TV series *Heartbeat* and as the bewitching Hogsmeade in *Harry Potter and the Philosopher's Stone*.

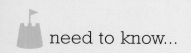 need to know...

SLEEP **Dillons of Whitby**, 14 Chubb Hill Road, is a centrally located, boutique-style bed and breakfast overlooking Pannett Park. It has five rooms, all of which have flat-screen TVs, iPod docks, Egyptian cotton linen and bathrobes are provided in the stylish bathrooms (01947 600290; www.dillonsofwhitby.co.uk). **Shoreline Cottages** offers more than 25 properties in Whitby, including two-bedroom Henrietta Cottage, which has a brick fireplace, beamed ceilings and a contemporary kitchen in a cobbled cul-de-sac just a few metres from the 199 steps (01904 607087; www.shoreline-cottages.com). **Abbey House**, East Cliff, has to be one of the best addresses in town. It is a newly refurbished youth hostel right next to the abbey, with spectacular views, family rooms and a restaurant serving dishes made from local produce (0845 3719049; www.yha.org.uk)

EAT **Botham's of Whitby**, 35–39 Skinner Street, offers treats such as home-made gingerbread with Wensleydale cheese, buttered plum bread and Bakewell tarts, which you can wash down with Yorkshire tea in this quintessentially English tea room (01947 602823; www.botham.co.uk). **Trenchers Seafood Restaurant**, New Quay Road, is another excellent fish and chip shop to rival the Magpie Café, but this one doesn't have the queues (01947 603212; www.trenchersrestaurant.co.uk). **The Black Horse**, 91 Church Street, is a 16th-century pub offering a Yorkshire cheese board and tapas (01947 602906; www.the-black-horse.com)

EXPLORE **Whitby Coastal Cruises** runs boat trips out on the bay and also whale-watching trips to spot minke and humpbacked whales from late summer into autumn. Trips depart from the boarding pontoon located at the Brewery Steps opposite the Lifeboat Station (01947 601385; www.whitbycoastalcruises.co.uk). Take a **bus** (www.arrivabus.co.uk) to Robin Hood's Bay (see page 44), explore the pretty stone fishing village and then **hike** along the 9.5-kilometre (6-mile) coastal path back to Whitby. **Hollin Equest**, Hollin Hall, Great Fryupdale, offers clients horse riding on the North York Moors (01947 897470; www.hollin equest.co.uk)

TOURIST INFORMATION **Whitby Tourist Information Centre**, Langborne Road (01723 383636). **www.visitwhitby.com**

GETTING THERE **Nearest train station** is Whitby (connections to Middlesbrough). **By road** Whitby is north of Scarborough off the A171

GOOD FOR Activity holidays, couples, families, walkers, wildlife enthusiasts

Morecambe Lancashire

The sun has set over a new-look Morecambe Bay. The reopening of the town's art deco icon, The Midland Hotel (www.midlandmorecambe.co.uk), marked the beginning of a new era for this Lancashire town, once the archetypal faded British seaside resort renowned for its crumbling arcades.

Noel Coward, Laurence Olivier and Coco Chanel all stayed at this art deco gem, designed by architect Oliver Hill to bend alongside the curve of the promenade, creating spectacular panoramas of the north-west coast. Today the revamped hotel, which reopened in summer 2008 after an £11-million refurbishment, also has a brand new upper floor with floor-to-ceiling windows to frame those stunning views and famous sunsets.

The Midland's beauty has returned with curving staircases, pewter handrails and Eric Gill sculptures adorning the walls and floors. Grainy

Anglers at Morecambe Bay, famed for its dramatic sunsets.

black-and-white photographs of heyday Morecambe with its lidos, bathing beauties and packed promenades are displayed on the walls. The 44 boutique-style rooms have fluffy bathrobes and posh toiletries in the sleek, modern bathrooms.

Art is a big part of the town's regeneration. The bollards lining the **Stone Jetty**, which juts out 800 metres (½ mile) into the Irish Sea, are topped with witty sculptures of seabirds, celebrating the abundant birdlife of Morecambe Bay. Steel cormorants, gannets and razorbills sit proudly on the roundabouts on **Central Drive** and on the top of sea railings.

On the **promenade** a bronze statue of a man doing a funny walk may also raise a smile. The town's most famous son, Eric Bartholomew – half of comedy double act Morecambe and Wise – took his stage name from the place where he grew up.

The Midland isn't the only landmark that has undergone an overhaul. Almost opposite the hotel is the Grade II listed Victoria Pavilion, better

The curvaceous art deco Midland Hotel stands proudly on the promenade.

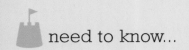

need to know...

ESSENTIAL • INFORMATION

SLEEP **The Clarendon Hotel**, Marine Road West, is a revamped three-star 19th-century hotel on the seafront with a traditional pub in the basement and a contemporary restaurant (see The Waterfront Restaurant below) (01524 410180; www.clarendon-hotel.co.uk). **Eden Vale Luxury Holiday Flats**, 338 Marine Road Central, is a Georgian house with seven self-catering flats sleeping two to four people (07946 021669). **The Inn at Whitewell** is a stone inn on the River Hodder, Forest of Bowland, with gorgeous rooms: antique furniture, peat fires and Victorian claw-foot baths. Also serves excellent food (01200 448222; www.innat whitewell.com)

EAT **The Waterfront Restaurant**, 74–76 Marine Road West, is a contemporary restaurant serving Morecambe Bay shrimps, steaks and grilled fish (01524 410180; www.the-waterfront-restaurant. co.uk). **Chill**, 228–229 Marine Road Central, a café on the seafront near the Stone Jetty, serves fresh fruit smoothies, home-made cakes and has jazz and blues nights (01524 424381). **Artisan**, 296 Marine Road Central, is a Slow Food proponent, so all the food is cooked fresh at this café where local artists' work adorns the walls (01524 417954)

EXPLORE Take a **train** from Morecambe to Ulverston in the Lake District: passing wetlands, coast, squat bridges; it's one of the most scenic rides in the country. **Ribble Bird Tours** offers a guided bird tour of Morecambe Bay (01253 312043; www.ribblebirdtours.co.uk). Cycle around the Forest of Bowland. **Cycle Adventure** offers bike hire and will deliver and collect from Morecambe/Forest of Bowland (07518 373007; www.cycle-adventure.co.uk)

TOURIST INFORMATION **Morecambe Visitor Information Centre**, Old Station Buildings, Marine Road Central (01524 582808; www.citycoast countryside.co.uk/site/morecambe-and-heysham)

GETTING THERE **Nearest train station** is Morecambe (connections to the mainline station at Lancaster). **By road** exit the M6 motorway at junction 34 and follow signs for Lancaster/ Morecambe

GOOD FOR Activity holidays, couples, families, wildlife enthusiasts

known as **Morecambe Winter Gardens** (www.thewintergardensmore cambe.co.uk), which reopened its doors in 2006 after nearly 30 years and is now putting on regular shows.

One perfectly preserved slice of the 1930s still going strong is the magnificent café **P. Brucciani** (01524 420676) on Marine Parade, a former milk bar with a brown wood and chrome exterior, red Formica tables and wall-to-wall etched glass of Venetian canal scenes. In summer it still serves that most art deco of confections, the Knickerbocker Glory.

Even the traditional ice-cream van has had a revamp. Walk along the promenade and you may spot a beautifully restored, pink classic Bedford CF van. **Sunset Ices** (www.everyday-is-like-sundae.co.uk) sells locally produced ice cream in traditional 99s, waffle cones and oysters.

On warm days the van probably does a roaring trade outside **Happy Mount Park**, on the eastern end of the promenade, which buzzes with families enjoying the trampolines, miniature railway, swing boats and the new Aqua Park where kids can splash about in the fountains.

Walk or cycle along the 8-kilometre (5-mile) stretch of promenade to **Heysham**, a pretty village with a tiny 14th-century cliff-top church, St Peter's, and Heysham Nature Reserve (although you can't miss the nearby power station).

Morecambe also makes an excellent base for touring the **Lake District** and the **Forest of Bowland** (www.forestofbowland.com) – an area of Outstanding Natural Beauty with heather moorland, blanket bog and rare birds – both within a 20-minute drive.

You can't visit Morecambe and not explore the bay, home to 200,000 wading birds and the third most important estuary in Europe. One of the best places to see the birds is at **Hest Bank**, a popular starting point for the **Cross Bay** walks (www.citycoastcountryside.co.uk), 13-kilometre (8-mile) guided treks across the bay.

ABOVE: *One of the town's new witty bird sculptures.*

BELOW: *Silverdale and Morecambe Bay from Arnside Knott, Cumbria.*

St Bees Cumbria

This small village, just 64.5 kilometres (40 miles) south of the England–Scotland border, is proof that there are parts of the Lake District that are still firmly off the tourist trail.

RIGHT: *Sunset over St Bees Head.*

The wide beach stretches for 1.5 kilometres (1 mile), with plenty of sand for castle building and a gently sloping shoreline, usually free from strong currents, making it perfect for old-fashioned family days on the beach. There is also a wide promenade, giving good disabled access, and an excellent children's play area.

Aside from the beach, the village itself is best known for its 400-year-old **St Bees School** and the impressive **Priory of St Mary and St Bega**, which was founded almost 1,000 years ago. St Bees is also renowned in walking circles as the start of the 306-kilometre (190-mile) Cross-England Coast to Coast Walk (made famous by Alfred Wainwright), ending in Robin Hood's Bay (see page 44) on the east coast but there are plenty of shorter circular walks from the village, ranging from around 3–8 kilometres (2–5 miles) in length. One of the most dramatic is along the clifftop path to **Fleswick Cove**. Tucked between two headlands, it is a shingle beach with beautiful pebbles and stones that people come to the beach to collect.

The easiest walk from the village is the climb up on to **St Bees Head** – a red sandstone bluff rising to over 91.5 metres (300 feet) – one of the most dramatic natural features on the whole of the north-west coast. An RSPB reserve on the headland is home to the only colony of black guillemots in England and there are observation points to watch the puffins, terns and other seabirds all along the headland. At nesting times, the cliffs and skies are full of kittiwakes, gulls and razorbills.

Although the beach at St Bees is stunning, it's impossible to be in this part of the world and not explore the tranquil landscapes of the **Lake District**. The nearby town of **Egremont** is situated at the foot of the Dent Fell and Udale Valley, and is steeped in history. It dates back to the

Wastwater Lake is owned by the National Trust.

RIGHT: Dramatic spring tide at St Bees.

13th century when the castle, now an atmospheric ruin, was originally built. Beyond it lie the stunning peaks of **Scafell**, **Great Gable** and **Wasdale**, overlooking Wastwater, the deepest lake in England. This is fantastic walking country or just laze around and take in the views.

The village itself has a clutch of shops, pubs and cafés but at its heart this is a peaceful, away-from-it-all kind of place. For somewhere a little more lively, the elegant Georgian town of **Whitehaven** is just a short drive away with a bustling marina and an enjoyable wet-weather attraction, **The Rum Story** (www.rumstory.co.uk). It is set in an original 18th-century warehouse and shop of a local family of rum producers, with interactive exhibits on the Caribbean, Africa and a slave ship. **The Beacon** museum (www.thebeacon-whitehaven.co.uk) on the harbourside is another great wet-weather option, with interactive exhibits on the history of the town.

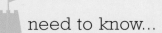

need to know...

ESSENTIAL · INFORMATION ·

SLEEP **Queens Hotel**, Main Street, is a cosy country pub in the heart of the village with oak beams, log fires and comfortable bedrooms (01946 822287; www.queenshotelstbees.co.uk). **Abbey Farm** offers comfortable, country-chic rooms on a former farm on the outskirts of the village and slap-up breakfasts (01946 823534; www.abbey farm-stbees.co.uk). **Seacote Park** combines a campsite, static vans and space for caravans and motorhomes, all overlooking the beach (01946 822777; www.seacote.com)

EAT **Hartley's Beach Shop and Café**, Beach Road, pop in for a legendary Hartley's ice cream. The Hartley family has been making ice cream for 70 years and now produces an amazing 50 different flavours at their creamery in Egremont (01946 820175). **Good Companions**, Seaview Nurseries, Nethertown, a short drive from St Bees, serves fantastic wood-fired pizzas for lunch and

dinner (01946 823324; www.goodcompanions restaurant.co.uk). **Zest Restaurant**, Low Road, Whitehaven, is one of the best-known restaurants in the area and serves up brasserie dishes to the likes of Tony Blair (01946 692848; www.zest whitehaven.com)

EXPLORE Cumbria offers some of the best **walking** in the UK; download routes (www.lake districtoutdoors.co.uk). **Riptide Boat Trips**, Whitehaven, offers three-hour boat trips to see birds and dolphins (01946 822679; www.white haven.org.uk/riptide.html)

TOURIST INFORMATION **www.stbees.org.uk/**

GETTING THERE Nearest train station is St Bees. **By road** St Bees is on the B5345, off the A595

GOOD FOR Families, walkers, wildlife enthusiasts

Southwold Suffolk

This well-heeled resort on Suffolk's Heritage Coast is quintessentially English, evoking idyllic childhood holidays spent on the pier, watching Punch and Judy shows and building sandcastles in front of a promenade lined with beach huts.

RIGHT: Southwold's main beach is a mix of sand and shingle.

BELOW: The Sole Bay Inn, in front of the squat lighthouse, serves locally brewed Adnams ale.

All of these things are still here today; it is a perfectly preserved piece of old-fashioned seaside escapism.

The recently restored **pier** (www.southwoldpier.co.uk) was built in 1900 as a landing stage for steamships that travelled up the coast from London Bridge at a time when most holidaymakers arrived by sea. Today you won't find any noisy fruit machines in the amusement arcades, just the traditional two-pence pushers, air hockey and racing horses. Tuck into everything from fish and chips to more fancy dishes such as pan-fried mackerel with a warm chorizo and potato salad in **The Clockhouse**, one of the pier's three restaurants. Four shops sell beach paraphernalia along with nautical gifts, chic homeware and ceramics.

The pier also has its fair share of quirky attractions such as **Under the Pier** (www.underthepier.com), a collection of handmade slot machines, a Mobility Masterclass where you can test your ability on a walking frame and a dog's eye view of Southwold. On the **promenade**, an eco-friendly fantastical clock, using water pumped from the pond and recycled copper, strikes every half an hour with all sorts of entertaining results.

Next to the pier is the town's main **beach**, a mix of sand and shingle with summer lifeguards and the painted beach huts in myriad colours, some available for day hire (www.southwoldhuts.co.uk). A special area of the beach is reserved for water sports including waterskiing and windsurfing, while fishing, with a permit, is allowed from the pier. If you prefer your beaches to be more remote, head to the sand-dune lined **Denes** close to the mouth of the River Blyth.

As well as its retro Victorian pier and iconic beach huts, Southwold also has another distinctive landmark, its squat **lighthouse** (www.trinityhouse.co.uk). Built in the late 19th century following 283

Southwold's retro pier offers traditional amusements.

shipwrecks in Sole Bay, it is now open for tours from Easter to early November. If you want to discover more about the town's links with the sea visit the fascinating **Southwold Museum** (www.southwoldmuseum.org) on Victoria Street, where you can learn about the explosive 132-ship and 50,000-men Battle of Sole Bay, fought just off the coast in 1672.

This pint-pot town is the perfect place for some idle wandering past pink-washed cottages, elegant Georgian houses and greens, which were left undeveloped to act as firebreaks after much of the town was lost in a disastrous fire in 1659. It's also retail heaven with smart interior shops, boutiques and a refreshing number of independent stores including a fishmonger, butcher and deli. Kids will go goggle-eyed over the acid drops and bullseyes among 150-odd traditional sweets crammed into jars at the corner shop, **One St James Green** (01502 726039).

The pubs are one of Southwold's biggest draws, serving up a perfectly warm pint of the local Adnams ale in atmospheric surroundings. **The Crown Hotel** (www.adnams.co.uk), **The Swan Hotel** and **The Lord Nelson** are all excellent, the latter retaining traces of a smugglers' passageway leading to the cliffs.

The sleepy seaside village of **Walberswick** makes a nice day trip. A small ferry takes boatloads of people there from Southwold Harbour during the summer. Just south of here is the **Walberswick National Nature Reserve** (www.naturalengland.org.uk), part of the largest freshwater reedbed in Britain. Keep a look out for otters, deer and rare butterflies.

RIGHT: Colourful beach huts line the promenade.

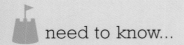

ESSENTIAL • INFORMATION

SLEEP **The Swan Hotel**, Market Place, owned by the Adnams brewery, has 42 rooms, the most stylish being the lighthouse rooms (01502 722186; www.adnams.co.uk). **Newlands**, Halesworth Road, Reydon, is a family-friendly bed and breakfast with an indoor pool and eight bedrooms, four of which are in a garden annexe 01502 722164; www.newlandsofsouthwold.co.uk). **Sweet Briar Cottage**, Eastbridge, an 11.5 kilometre (7-mile) drive from Southwold, is an upmarket thatched cottage sleeping six (01386 701177; www.rural retreats.co.uk)

EAT **The Swan Hotel**, Market Place, is the place to eat in Southwold, with fresh local fish complemented by a great wine list (01502 722186; www.adnams.co.uk). **The Lord Nelson**, East Street, serves enormous portions of fish and chips, game pies and home-made curries (01502 722079; www.thelordnelsonsouthwold.co.uk). **Boardwalk Café**, on the pier, offers excellent cream teas plus early-evening fish and chips, all served up with sea views (01502 722105; www.southwoldpier.co.uk)

EXPLORE **Coastal Voyager**, office at the harbour, offers a range of nautical trips: a leisurely river cruise up the River Blyth to spot marsh harriers and herons; a three-hour high-speed trip to see the grey and common seals at Scroby Sands; a 30-minute high-speed blast around Sole Bay (07887 525082; www.coastalvoyager.co.uk). **Electric Picture Palace**, Blackmill Road, is a 66-seater cinema, opened in 2002 but designed in a 1912 traditional style with a tiny Wurlitzer organ. Shows an eclectic selection of films (07815 769565; www.exploresouthwold.co.uk/cinema/). **Africa Alive**, White's Lane, Kessingland, is a coastal safari park near Lowestoft, perfect for a

day trip with the kids (01502 740291; www.africa-alive.co.uk). **Moo Play Farm**, Low Farm, Locks Road, Brampton, has an indoor play barn and outdoor adventure play farm, kids can pet an alpaca, ponies, goats and pigs and take a tractor ride (01502 575841; www.mooplayfarm.co.uk)

TOURIST INFORMATION **Southwold Tourist information Centre**, High Street (01502 724729; www.visit-sunrisecoast.co.uk)

GETTING THERE **Nearest train stations** are Darsham and Halesworth (14.5 kilometres (9 miles) from Southwold). **By road** take the main A12 coastal road, then the A1095 into Southwold

GOOD FOR Couples, families, walkers, wildlife enthusiasts

Holkham Norfolk

It's the vast expanse of sea, sky and sand that make this stretch of beach fringed with pine trees so enticing.

RIGHT: Holkham Hall is set in extensive grounds.

People don't come here for the swimming. In low tide, when the beach is 800 metres (½ mile) deep, it can take a frustrating 20 minutes to reach the water. Don't expect lifeguards or beachfront facilities either. Holkham is best for simple pleasures such as sandcastle building, kite flying and birdwatching. In winter there's nothing like a bracing walk along the sand with the North Sea breeze stinging your face before retiring to a cosy pub.

Holkham Beach is great for bracing winter walks.

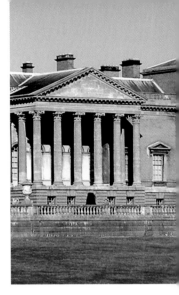

Day-trippers tend to base themselves close to the car-park end of the beach but it's more rewarding to keep going through the pinewoods into the wider reaches of the dunes where it's more secluded and you'll feel like you're on the moon. The Queen, when staying at nearby Sandringham, is believed to exercise her corgis on the beach. Holkham also gained worldwide acclaim after appearing in the closing scene of *Shakespeare in Love* when a lonely, windswept Gwyneth Paltrow walks to the water's edge.

Bring your binoculars if you want to fully appreciate the abundant wildlife. The beach is part of the **Holkham National Nature Reserve**,

stretching from Burnham Norton to Blakeney and covering 4,000 hectares (9,884 acres), criss-crossed by footpaths. You don't even have to step out of the beach car park to see hordes of wildfowl; pink-footed, white-fronted and brent geese often congregate in the adjoining fields.

The western end of the beach is a nudist section. Head east and you will reach **Wells-next-the-Sea**, an ancient fishing port where daily catches of crab are still landed on the quayside and pretty, coloured beach huts on stilts sit among the sand dunes.

If you crave some lush, rural scenery stroll through the grounds of **Holkham Hall** (www.holkham.co.uk), a grand Palladian mansion in a deer park designed by Capability Brown, with mature trees and an ornamental lake. Don't miss touring the brick mansion, home of the Coke family and the Earls of Leicester, with its sumptuous interior dripping with gilt, tapestries and fine furniture. It's open on selected days between Easter and October while the park opens every day except Christmas Day. Holkham village is built either side of the grand drive leading to the park and has a tea room, café and shop, selling everything from estate venison and wild game to home-made ice cream including unusual flavours such as lavender, fig and plum.

A windmill at sunset at Burnham Overy.

Just opposite is the estate-owned **The Victoria** hotel, which attracts weekending Londoners wanting luxury and good food with their windswept views. Another 'Chelsea-on-Sea' enclave is **Burnham Market**, a gentrified but achingly pretty village with fine Georgian buildings clustered around the green and a vast array of smart interior shops, designer boutiques and delis. It's also home to the 17th-century **Hoste Arms** (www.hostearms.co.uk), a gastropub with 35 stylish rooms, famed for establishing Norfolk's foodie reputation. It's also popular with locals, who prop up the bar.

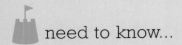
need to know...

SLEEP **The Victoria**, Park Road, has individually designed opulent rooms with exotic fabrics, some with four-posters and roll-top baths. Three characterful self-catering lodges are dotted around the estate (01328 711008; www.holkham.co.uk/victoria/). **The White Horse**, Brancaster Staithe, has 15 contemporary rooms overlooking the salt marshes (01485 210262; www.whitehorse brancaster.co.uk). **Deepdale Tipis and Yurts**, Deepdale Farm, Burnham Deepdale, provides you with the opportunity to enjoy a night under canvas with a difference (01485 210256; www.deepdale farm.co.uk)

EAT **The White Horse**, Brancaster Staithe, has a conservatory and wooden deck overlooking the salt marshes and Scolt Head Island. Tuck into oysters, mussels, cockles and samphire sourced within 137 metres (150 yards) (01485 210262; www.whitehorsebrancaster.co.uk). **Deepdale Café**, Main Road, Burnham Deepdale, serves locally smoked haddock and kippers, full English fry-up with local sausages and organic eggs, Sunday roast; or just pop in for a sandwich and café latte (01485 211055; www.deepdalecafe.co.uk). **Titchwell Manor**, Titchwell (near Brancaster), is a Victorian hotel next to Titchwell Marsh Nature Reserve. It serves up Brancaster oysters, locally smoked salmon and roast loin of venison (01485 210221; www.titchwellmanor.com)

EXPLORE Take a **ferry** from Burnham Overy Staithe to Scolt Head Island, a wildfowl reserve with creeks and marshes that's perfect for a picnic and a swim. The ferry runs from April to October (01485 210456). **On Yer Bike**, The Laurels, Nutwood Farm, Wighton, hires out bikes. Head inland to discover the brick and flint villages such as Binham, with its pretty green and great pub, The Chequers Inn, and Walsingham with its ruined abbey and tea rooms (01328 820719; www.norfolk cyclehire.co.uk). **Thursford Collection,** Thursford (near Fakenham) is great for a family day out. It is home to the world's largest collection of steam engines and organs. Ride on fairground carousels or let the kids run off some of their own steam in the adventure playground (01328 878477; www. thursford.com)

TOURIST INFORMATION
www.visitnorthnorfolk.com

GETTING THERE **Nearest train station** is King's Lynn (37 kilometres (23 miles) from Holkham). **By road** Holkham is 3 kilometres (2 miles) west of Wells-next-the-Sea on the A149 coastal road

GOOD FOR Couples, families, peace and quiet, walkers, wildlife enthusiasts

Blakeney Norfolk

Visit the North Norfolk coast in winter and you may witness an amazing aerial display. It won't be the Red Arrows performing a fly-past but a skein of pink-footed geese.

There may be tens of thousands of them, swarming across the sky en route to the salt marshes where they roost. It's not an uncommon sight on this stretch of coastline, which is blessed with abundant nature reserves such as **Blakeney Point**. This is an internationally renowned coastal reserve with salt marshes and sand dunes that attract a huge variety of migratory birds.

National Trust-run Blakeney Point, an Area of Outstanding Natural Beauty, is also a favourite basking and breeding point for some 500 common and grey seals along its 5.5-kilometre (3½-mile) long sand and shingle spit. The best way to see them is to take an hour-long boat trip from Blakeney or Morston Quay with one of the three family-run firms: **Beans Boat Trips** (www.beansboattrips.co.uk), **Temples Seal Trips** (www.sealtrips.co.uk) and **Bishop's Boats** (www.norfolksealtrips.co.uk). Common seals have their young between June and August, the greys between November and January. The inquisitive creatures often pop up and swim around the tour boats. Watch out for common, sandwich and little terns running along the shore where they lay their eggs. During the winter you will see large numbers of geese including pink-footed and brent geese, which arrive in the autumn from cooler climes such as Greenland.

The pretty village of **Blakeney**, once a busy fishing and trading port before the harbour silted up, is typical of this stretch of flat coastline, with its traditional flint cottages, Dutch gabled buildings (a legacy from when the area had close trading ties with the Netherlands), cosy pubs and broad sweeps of sea, saltings and sky. A harbour still caters for boats small enough to navigate the River Glaven.

The charming seaside town of **Wells-Next-the-Sea** is 9.5 kilometres (6 miles) west of Blakeney. It is famous for its brightly coloured beach

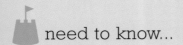

SLEEP Blakeney Hotel overlooks the quay and has great views over the estuary and salt marshes. This 60-room hotel is family-friendly (01263 740797; www.blakeney-hotel.co.uk). **Cley Windmill**, Cley-next-the-Sea, is a local landmark that has been converted into a stylish guesthouse with self-catering accommodation in the adjoining stables. Dinner available (01263 740209; www.cleywindmill.co.uk). **Byfords**, 1–3 Shirehall Plain, Holt, is a posh bed and breakfast with boutique hotel-style rooms: Egyptian cotton sheets, DVD, TV and sound systems and stylish bathrooms. Downstairs is a bustling café, which sells giant slabs of home-made cake and turns into a relaxed bistro in the evening (01263 711400; www.byfords.org.uk)

EAT The Moorings, High Street, serves unpretentious food – lots of local game and fish – in a relaxed setting (01263 740054; www.blakeney-moorings.co.uk). **Morston Hall**, Morston, serves Michelin-starred food within an elegant country

house hotel 1.5 kilometres (1 mile) from the coast. Try roast tail of monkfish followed by champagne jelly with strawberry ripple ice cream (01263 741041; www.morstonhall.com). **Walsingham Farm Shop**, Guild Street, Little Walsingham, offers local pies, honey and beers (01328 821877; www.walsinghamfarmshop.co.uk); close to the farm shop you'll find their family-friendly and contemporary sister restaurant **The Norfolk Riddle** and an excellent fish and chip shop takeaway counter, which uses local potatoes and sustainable fish (01328 821903)

EXPLORE Charlie Ward Traditional Boats, Morston, offers charter trips in a traditional sailing barge, which can sail along tidal creeks or the coast (01263 740377; www.charlieward-trad-boats.co.uk). **The Bird ID Company** offers seasonal bird tours. Spot cranes, geese and owls in winter or waders in the summer (01603 440907; www.birdtour.co.uk). **Norfolk Fishing Trips & Charter** will take you to prime fishing spots. Fish for mackerel, cod and bass. Based in Brancaster Staithe in summer and Lowestoft Marina in winter (01485 512474; www.norfolkfishingtrips.co.uk)

TOURIST INFORMATION Wells-Next-the-Sea Tourist Information Centre, Staithe Street (01328 710885). **www.visitnorthnorfolk.com**

GETTING THERE Nearest train station is either King's Lynn (53 kilometres (33 miles) from Blakeney) or Norwich (57 kilometres (35½ miles) from Blakeney). **By road** Blakeney is off the A149 between King's Lynn and Cromer

GOOD FOR Activity holidays, couples, families, peace and quiet, wildlife enthusiasts

huts on stilts lining the dune-backed sand, reached via a narrow gauge railway. Wander around the old town, which has Georgian houses and flint cottages surrounding the green or take a 30-minute train ride on the narrow gauge steam railway to **Little Walsingham** (www.wells walsinghamrailway.co.uk).

North Norfolk has a few bucket-and-spade resorts, such as **Cromer**, a once fashionable Victorian holiday destination now home to the UK's only remaining traditional end-of-the-pier variety show. There is a safe, sandy, Blue Flag beach, amusement arcades and plenty of fish and chip shops. And you can't visit without sampling Cromer's famous crab.

If you fancy a change of scene, drive inland to **Holt Country Park** (01263 516062), a 40.5-hectare (100-acre) woodland with waymarked trails, a children's play area and small visitor centre. Stately home fans will enjoy **Blickling Hall, Gardens and Park** (www.nationaltrust.org.uk), one of England's great Jacobean houses, with year-round interest in the glorious gardens. **Felbrigg Hall, Garden and Park** (www.nationaltrust.org.uk) with its imposing Georgian drawing room, Gothic-style library and extensive gardens and park, is also worth a visit.

There are also plenty of family-friendly attractions around including **Amazona Zoo** (www.amazonazoo.co.uk) in Cromer. **Cromer Lifeboat Station** (www.cromerlifeboats.org.uk) can be visited by groups but must be booked at least one week in advance. **Bewilderwood** (www.bewilderwood.co.uk) in Hoveton is a treehouse adventure with zip wires and jungle bridges. However, for just as much fun, and it has the added bonus of being free, take them crabbing on **Blakeney Quay**.

LEFT: Seals at Blakeney Point; they often pop up and swim around the tour boats.

Old boat on the salt marshes at Blakeney.

Aldeburgh Suffolk

A popular destination for seafood and music lovers, this pretty coastal town still feels remarkably untouched by modern-day life. Fishing boats are hauled up the shingle beach where ramshackle huts sell the fresh-from-the-nets catch.

RIGHT: Elegant guesthouses and pastel-coloured cottages line the promenade at Aldeburgh.

The surrounding area is mostly nature reserves while the promenade with its pastel-coloured cottages and elegant guesthouses seems little changed since Victorian times.

Today it has a reputation for its **annual music festival** (www. aldeburgh.co.uk), held every June and first launched by composer Benjamin Britten in 1948. A controversial 3.5-metre (12-foot) high steel sculpture, **The Scallop**, honouring him stands at the northern end of this unspoilt shingle beach where he once enjoyed an afternoon stroll. He is buried in the town's **St Peter and St Paul's Church** on Victoria Road.

The town also has bookshops, boutiques, an old-fashioned sweet shop and a half-timbered cinema that also serves as an art gallery.

Fishing boats are still hauled up the shingle beach at Aldeburgh.

You can learn more about the town's history at **The Aldeburgh Museum** (www.aldeburghmuseum.org.uk), housed in the 400-year-old timber-framed Moot Hall. Back in the 16th century the town was a thriving port with a flourishing shipbuilding industry (Sir Francis Drake's *Golden Hind*, first called *Pelican*, was built here) but when the River Alde silted up it went into decline. Coastal erosion also meant it lost the heart of its old town, only retaining Moot Hall, the Norman church and the **Martello Tower at Slaughden**, built as a fort during the Napoleonic wars and now available for holiday rents through the Landmark Trust (www.landmarktrust.org.uk).

Suffolk's east coast has taken quite a battering from the sea with the once-thriving port town of **Dunwich**, where churches and hundreds of houses were swept away, now a quiet village.

RIGHT: The House in the Clouds in Thorpeness is available to rent.

Orford, 21.5 kilometres (13½ miles) south of Aldeburgh, is well worth a visit with its castle (www.english-heritage.org.uk) and magnificent Norman keep. Climb 200 steps to the top for spectacular coastal views. Between April and October you can catch a ferry to National Trust-run **Orford Ness** (www.nationaltrust.org.uk), once used as a secret military test site, it is the largest vegetated shingle spit in Europe with rare wading birds, animals and plants. The Royal Society for the Protection of Birds' (RSPB) flagship reserve **Minsmere** (www.rspb.org.uk), near Aldeburgh, is also a must for bird lovers. It has a hide where you can see the constant comings and goings of migrant birds.

Don't miss **Thorpeness**. It's not every day you see a seven-storey half-timbered folly. It is now called the **House in the Clouds** (www.houseintheclouds.co.uk) and is available to rent. Britain's first purpose-built holiday village was dreamt up in 1912 by the playwright and barrister Glencairn Stuart Ogilvie. Today you can wander past houses with black wooden beams and white rendering, a windmill and take a rowing boat on the Meare, a huge, hand-dug lake with islands. There's also a lovely sand and shingle beach.

Fishermen sell their freshly caught fish from ramshackle huts on Aldeburgh beach.

Take a bracing walk along the **Suffolk Coast and Heaths Path** (www.suffolkcoastandheaths.org), which passes around 800 metres (½ mile) north of Aldeburgh. Or walk 5 kilometres (3 miles) inland via woods and fields to **Snape** with its Victorian maltings buildings (where barley was once malted), nestled alongside the River Alde with shops, galleries, restaurants and the world-famous concert hall (www.snapemaltings.co.uk). From here you can take boat trips along the river or join one of the RSPB's guided bird walks where you may spot a flash of electric blue, a kingfisher.

If it's fresh fish you want **Aldeburgh** is the only place to go. After a drink in the **White Hart Inn** (01728 453205) on High Street, where fishermen rub shoulders with weekenders, pop next door to the family-run **Aldeburgh Fish and Chip Shop** (01728 454685). Be prepared to queue; the succulent battered fish and crisp chips draw quite a crowd.

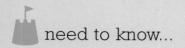

EAT **The Lighthouse Restaurant**, 77 High Street, serves homely dishes in a bistro-style setting. Excellent fish (01728 453377; www.lighthouse restaurant.co.uk). **Café 152**, 152 High Street, is a friendly restaurant that has developed an excellent reputation for its simply cooked fish, from chargrilled squid to grilled sole (01728 454594). **Butley Orford Oysterage**, Market Square, Orford, specializes in freshly caught fish from its own boats and hot-smoked eel, trout and mackerel from its own smokehouse. The restaurant and shop are situated next to each other (01394 450277; www.butleyorfordoysterage.co.uk)

EXPLORE Take a 30-minute river trip up the Alde from Snape (www.snapemaltings.co.uk). **MV *Lady Florence*** is a 12-passenger, wooden, Second World War supply ship. It can be booked for a leisurely brunch, lunch or dinner cruise. The cruises operate year-round from Orford Quay and the food is cooked fresh onboard using local produce (07831 698298; www.lady-florence.co.uk). **RSPB** offers a guided walk along the Alde Estuary or you can spot hunting barn owls, kestrels and wading birds through telescopes at the Snape Wildlife Information Centre (01728 687192; www. rspb.org.uk)

SLEEP **The Brudenell**, The Parade, is a 42-room traditional Edwardian hotel on the seafront with great seascapes and friendly staff (01728 452071; www.brudenellhotel.co.uk). **Ocean House**, 25 Crag Path, is a Victorian guesthouse with wrap-around sea views and rooms done out in period style (01728 452094; www.oceanhousealdeburgh. co.uk). **Aldeburgh Cottage**, High Street, is a stylish, self-catering, two-bedroom, 19th-century cottage with garden (01728 638962; www. aldeburghcottage.co.uk)

TOURIST INFORMATION Aldeburgh Tourist Information Centre, 152 High Street (01728 453637). **www.visitaldeburgh.co.uk**

GETTING THERE **Nearest train station** is Saxmundham (12 kilometres (7.5 miles) from Aldeburgh). **By road** Aldeburgh is off the A12

GOOD FOR Couples, families, peace and quiet, walkers, wildlife enthusiasts

Barafundle Bay Pembrokeshire

The joy of the beach at Barafundle is that it is just that: a beach. There are no sunloungers, ice-cream kiosks, deckchairs, jet skis or beach huts to interrupt the view. Instead there is just a blisteringly beautiful stretch of golden sand, backed by dunes and pine trees.

RIGHT: The tranquil beach at Stackpole.

The area is so deliciously unspoilt that it almost feels like a Caribbean beach yet to be discovered. Located 800 metres' (½ mile's) walk from the nearest car park, its isolated location is part of the reason why it remains so untouched. Go any time outside of high season and you may have the beach almost to yourself.

Steps lead down the cliff from the car park, which make the beach inaccessible to wheelchair users and buggies. It's worth remembering that everything you take down to the beach has to be brought back up. Once there the sea is sparklingly clean and ideal for swimming. When the tide is out there are caves to explore and from the centre of the bay there are stunning views across to **Lundy Island**.

Sandcastle building on Barafundle Beach.

The beach is part of a 13-kilometre (8-mile) stretch of coast owned by the National Trust known as **Stackpole** (www.nationaltrust.org.uk), which encompasses the small villages of Stackpole Quay and Bosherston, the nature reserve at Bosherston Lakes and another stunning beach at Broadhaven. All are linked by the **Pembrokeshire Coastal Path** (www.pcnpa.org.uk), making it easy to explore on foot as there are clearly waymarked paths. There are picturesque walks through the **Stackpole Woodlands** – once the grounds of a grand stately home that was long since demolished – and past the beautiful lily ponds at Bosherston. The coastal path to **Trewent** is particularly spectacular, passing an impressive fort at **Greenala** and giving dramatic views of the cliffs that dominate this stretch of coastline.

Stackpole Quay is the nearest village to Barafundle. Just 800 metres (½ mile) away, it boasts one of the smallest harbours in the country, with barely room for two boats. It's an idyllic spot, with just a tea room, a

The cliffs above Stackpole Bay.

clutch of pleasure boats to hire and picturesque cottages, which are also owned by the National Trust and can be rented as holiday homes.

Bosherston is a short drive inland from the beach and is dominated by its three beautiful lakes, often filled with water lilies. Originally created in the 18th century as coarse-fishing lakes, they have been turned into a nature reserve and are now home to otters as well as dozens of different bird species. It's still possible to fish the lakes but simply strolling beside them – particularly when the lilies are in flower in late spring and early summer – is a pleasure all of its own.

If you're after a beach with a few more facilities, the sprawling sands at **Broadhaven** have parking close by, a café and all manner of watersports. It's worth paying a visit to this busy stretch of beach just to be able to return to Barafundle and take even greater delight in its unspoilt charms.

RIGHT: The sparkling sands of Barafundle Beach.

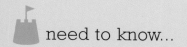 need to know...

SLEEP The Stackpole Inn, Jasons Corner, Stackpole, has four sleek rooms and is in an ideal location just 15 minutes' walk from the beach (01646 672324; www.stackpoleinn.co.uk). **Quay Cottage** 1/2, Stackpole Quay, is a pair of pretty two-bedroom cottages. Each sleeps three plus a cot and has a small garden; owned by the National Trust (0844 8002070; www.nationaltrustcottages. co.uk). **Freshwater East Caravan Club Site**, Trewent Hill, is a short drive away from Barafundle with good facilities and only a few minutes' walk from a stunning stretch of beach (01646 672341)

EAT St Govan's Country Inn, Bosherston, offers good pub food and well-kept ales. Accommodation also available (01646 661311). **Boathouse Tearoom**, Stackpole Quay, is a great spot for afternoon tea and cake (01646 672672). **The Stackpole Inn** is one of the best places in the area to eat, with freshly caught fish served up every day (see above)

EXPLORE Pembrokeshire Coastal Path links the villages and beaches (www.pcnpa.org.uk). **Stackpole Centre for Outdoor Learning**, National Trust, Old Home Farmyard, Stackpole, offers a range of activities – kayaking, coasteering, biking and walking – for families (01646 661464; www. stackpole.org.uk)

TOURIST INFORMATION
www.visitpembrokeshire.com

GETTING THERE Nearest train station is Pembroke (8 kilometres (5 miles) from Barafundle Bay). **By road** take the B4319 from Pembroke and follow signs to Stackpole

GOOD FOR Activity holidays, couples, families, wildlife enthusiasts

Llanbedrog Gwynedd

The sleepy village and beautiful beach at Llanbedrog lie at the heart of the wild and unspoilt Lleyn Peninsula; a dramatic spit of land on the north-west coast of Wales, where mountains fall away into the sea and the countryside is dotted with whitewashed farms, Iron Age forts and glorious wide bays edged with white sand.

RIGHT: Low tide at Llanbedrog, with views to Snowdonia.

Llanbedrog boasts just such a beach, backed by picturesque, multicoloured beach huts and dominated by a wooded headland at its southern end. The sand slopes gently into the water, making it ideal for younger families and offering safe swimming.

The village of Llanbedrog clambers up the hillside. It is a gentle kind of place, unspoilt by tourism, where the air is filled with voices talking in Welsh and the sense that 21st-century life has yet to arrive. Split into two by a main road, the beach is within walking distance from the lower part of the village, which is also where many other enjoyable local walking routes begin.

The upper part of the village stretches up the hill and is the livelier of the two, home to two pubs and a village shop. Along with the beach, the village is most famous for the **Oriel Plas Glyn-y-Weddw** (www. oriel.org.uk), originally built in the 1850s to house the art collection of Lady Elizabeth Love Jones Parry, a wealthy widow. The house itself is beautiful, with a dramatic Jacobean staircase and 10 large gallery spaces that now house paintings and sculptures by a variety of artists. There are constantly changing exhibitions, workshops, lectures and a fantastic gallery shop.

Pleasures on the **Lleyn Peninsula** are of the simple kind; lazing on the beach, walking across the neat farmers' fields, spotting the rare birds that nest on the ledges of the highest cliffs. If a stroll along the beach whets your appetite for a longer walk there's an excellent circular route beginning at the National Trust car park that heads up

on to **Mynydd Tir y Cwmwd**, an area of open moorland that climbs to 132 metres (433 feet), and offers great views along the coastline before coming back along the beach. It's around 8 kilometres (5 miles) and crosses the **Lleyn Coastal Path**, which offers longer walks along the peninsula.

If you're after a little more life, the market town – and unofficial capital of the Lleyn Peninsula – **Pwllheli** is a short drive away. A new marina with some 400 berths has brought new life to the town and all manner of day boat trips are on offer from the harbour. **Abersoch**, to the south of Llanbedrog, is one of the biggest sailing towns in the whole of Wales and is a great place for a day trip, with boats whisking across the bay and a bustling harbour.

However, spending time on the Lleyn Peninsula is really all about getting back to nature, whether it's watching the dolphins and seals in the bay from one of the gorse-clad hillsides, swimming in the crystal sea or sitting in **The Galley** café (01758 740730) above Llanbedrog beach, watching the clouds scudding across the vast expanse of sky.

RIGHT: Colourful huts line the Llanbedrog beach.

Below: Set sail from Llanbedrog Beach.

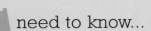

need to know...

SLEEP **Tremfan Hall** ticks the sleeping and eating boxes; elegant country-house rooms above a top-notch restaurant (01758 740169; www.tremfanhall.com). **Bolmynydd Camping Park** is a short stroll from Llanbedrog, with four camping fields and excellent facilities (07882 850820; www.bolmynydd.co.uk). **Wernfawr Manor Farm** is somewhere the kids will love staying as they can help feed the animals. Self-catering cottages and bed and breakfast in the farmhouse are both available (01758 740156; www.wernfawrmanorfarm.freeserve.co.uk)

EAT **The Galley**, Beach Road, is located right on the beach and is a must-visit. Booking for dinner is essential (01758 740730). **The Ship Inn** does standard pub food but has an excellent play area for children and is extremely welcoming to families (01758 741111; www.theshipinn.org.uk). **Caffi'r Oriel**, Oriel Plas Glyn-y-Weddw, is the tea rooms at the gallery (see above). Cake lovers should head here as home-made puddings and cakes are on offer each day (01758 740763; www.oriel.org.uk)

EXPLORE **Welsh Highland Heritage Railway** is the way to see the peninsula by train (01766 513402; www.whr.co.uk). **North Wales Fishing Charter**, Pwllheli, will take you out on a fishing trip to Bardesy Island (01286 882611; www.northwalesfishingcharter.com). **Lleyn Coastal Path** stretches for 152 kilometres (95 miles) around the peninsula (www.gwynedd.gov.uk)

TOURIST INFORMATION www.llynvisitor.co.uk

GETTING THERE **Nearest train station** is Pwllheli (6.5 kilometres (4 miles) from Llanbedrog). **By road** it is situated on the A499, south of Pwllheli

---

GOOD FOR Families, walkers, wildlife enthusiasts

St David's Pembrokeshire

On the very tip of West Wales, surrounded by the sea on three sides, the St David's Peninsula is steeped in history and is home to the smallest city in the UK and some of the country's most stunning beaches.

The village of **St David's** was awarded 'city' status due to its 12th-century cathedral, which became a popular place of pilgrimage in medieval times. The village also boasts a ruined 14th-century bishops' palace, a 13th-century tower gate and the very 21st-century Oriel y Parc art gallery.

The town is a perfect base for exploring the surrounding countryside. A morning lazing on the beach paired with an afternoon strolling around the galleries and craft shops that line its atmospheric streets is a perfect combination. **Oriel y Parc** (www.orielyparc.co.uk) on Caerfai Road is a new gallery and visitor centre that exhibits the work of local artists along with interactive exhibits and local information. **Hilton Court** (www.hilton gardensandcrafts.co.uk), approximately 16 kilometres (10 miles) to the south of St David's, is a group of restored stables that house local craftspeople – potters, painters and jewellery-makers. You can watch them at work as well as view and buy their wares. There are also 20 hectares (12 acres) of beautiful gardens.

The famous beach and coastline at Whitesands.

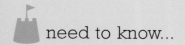

need to know...

SLEEP **Ramsey House**, Lower Moor, is the epitome of bed and breakfast chic in the heart of St David's. It has four sleek bedrooms with Designers Guild furniture, White Company toiletries and flat-screen TVs (01437 720321; www.ramsey house.co.uk). **The Grove**, High Street, is the place for foodies as in addition to the seven chic bedrooms it has an excellent restaurant (01437 720341; www.grovestdavids.co.uk). **Pencarnan Farm Caravan & Camping site**, located above Whitesands Bay, has great views and good facilities and is the best in what is a very popular camping area (01437 720580)

EAT **Cwtch**, 22 High Street, serves up locally produced lamb and beef, seafood and cheeses in a friendly, buzzy dining room (01437 720491; www.cwtchrestaurant.co.uk). **The Sampler**, 17 Nun Street, is where history and home-made cakes mix. There is a Home Front Experience exhibition in the cellar and home-made cakes, scones and sandwiches in the tea room upstairs. **The Sloop Inn**, Porthgain, does great pub food

and is ideal for families (01348 831449; www.sloop.co.uk)

EXPLORE **Venture Jet** offers a jet boat adventure trip from Whitesands along with wildlife- and whale-watching trips and high-speed adventures in its rigid inflatable boat (RIB) (01348 837764; www. venturejet.co.uk). **Thousand Island Expeditions**, booking office at lower end of Cross Square, runs boat trips to Ramsey Island, for which it has exclusive landing rights (01437 721721; www. thousandislands.co.uk)

TOURIST INFORMATION **www.stdavids.co.uk**. **www.visitpembrokeshire.com**

GETTING THERE **Nearest train station** is Haverfordwest (25.5 kilometres (16 miles) from St David's). **By road** follow the A40 to Haverfordwest and then take the A487 to St David's

GOOD FOR Activity holidays, couples, families, walkers, wildlife enthusiasts

There's plenty to explore in St David's but what draws most people to this area of Pembrokeshire is the breathtaking beaches. The entire coastal strip is part of the **Pembrokeshire Coast National Park** (www.pcnpa.org.uk), which runs an extensive programme of activities for children and adults, including walks, rock-pooling and even crab-catching.

The most famous beach on the Pembrokeshire coast is **Whitesands**, a 1.5-kilometre (1-mile) long stretch of golden sand that looks across to Ramsey Island and offers fantastic – and safe – surfing and swimming. In high season the beach does get crowded (and it can be worth the 2.5-kilometre (1½-mile) walk along the coast to **Porthmelgan**, which has no facilities and is always quiet) but at other times of the year it is truly spectacular. Other bays worth visiting are **Aberfelin** and **Abercastle**. All of the beaches are accessible along the **Pembrokeshire Coast Path** from St David's.

Walk the Pembrokeshire Coast Path.

This area is great for families with older children. The **Whitesands Surf School** (www.whitesandssurfschool) is excellent, and will keep teens happy, and kayaking, whitewater rafting and rock climbing are all on offer in the area. However, it is possible to escape to quieter corners. **Ramsey Island**, a short boat trip from nearby **St Justinian**, is an RSPB reserve that is home to a wide variety of bird life and the largest colony of grey seals in Britain. Days at sea can be easily organized, with a range of fishing boats offering day trips out of St David's.

The peninsula is renowned for its abundant wildlife. In autumn a walk along the Pembrokeshire Coast Path gives you the chance to see seal pups basking in some of the quiet coves and secluded bays. In spring, kittiwakes and shearwaters wheel in the skies above. This is fantastic walking country, with paths that wind past ancient sites and standing stones, testament to the spirituality of this isolated and beautiful peninsula.

LEFT: Take up surfing on St David's beach.

Rhossili Swansea

The Gower Peninsula in South Wales was the first area in the UK to be designated an Area of Outstanding Natural Beauty over 50 years ago. It has some of the country's most beautiful beaches, which are backed by unspoilt grassland, heath and oak woodland.

Rhossili Bay is the area's crowning glory; a long sweep of golden sand that stretches far off into the distance, broken only by the skeletal remains of shipwrecked boats and swept with dramatic waves that offer some of the best surfing in the region.

The village of **Rhossili** is a gateway to fantastic walking country and much of the land beyond it is owned by the National Trust (www.national trust.org.uk) – the Trust's shop and visitor centre in the town has plenty of local information. The high, open headland to the west of the village leads to **Worms Head**, a dramatic headland that itself leads on to two small islands, accessible by a causeway at low tide. It's well worth the walk for the astonishing views. If you make it to the second island, **Outer Head**, look out for cormorants circling in the sky above.

But the main draw in Rhossili is the glorious **beach** below. Once down the long flight of steps there are vast expanses of sand to explore.

Rhossili's golden arc of beach.

Take a fishing trip.

Mumbles pier was built in 1898 and has a pub, café and family entertainment centre.

Regular waves make it a popular surfing beach, with the best breaks towards the northern end at Llangennith. Kite surfing, canoeing and kayaking are also all on offer in the area. The dramatic landscapes lend themselves to adventure on land as well; the rugged limestone coast offers plentiful rock climbing and abseiling possibilities, as well as coasteering.

The village itself is steeped in history. The church has an arch above the door that dates back to the 12th century and is rumoured to have belonged to the 'lost village' that was built around 1100 before being buried by sandstorms in the 14th century. On **Rhossili Down** there are burial chambers dating back to the Bronze Age. An 8-kilometre (5-mile) circular walk over the down combines the ancient sites with glorious views. The walk starts from the **National Trust Rhossili Visitor Centre and Shop** (01792 390707), which is in Coastguard Cottages, on the tip of the Gower Peninsula, next to Rhossili beach.

Beyond Rhossili there are plenty more beaches to discover; the pretty bay at **Mewslade** is just 15 minutes' walk away, while nearby **Oxwich** has its own nature reserve. One of the richest coastal habitats in Britain,

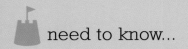

need to know...

SLEEP The Worms Head Hotel is perched above the bay and all rooms have glorious sea views (01792 390512; www.thewormshead.co.uk). **The Old Rectory**, Rhossili Bay, is a comfortable, four-bedroomed, self-catering cottage that has spectacular views across the bay (0844 8002070; www.nationaltrustcottages.co.uk). **Kennexstone Camping & Touring Park**, Llangennith, is the place that campers should head to. It has good facilities and is situated on a working organic farm (01792 386790; www.gowercamping.co.uk)

EAT The Bay Bistro offers great cream teas by day and Welsh Black steak or local seafood in the evenings (01792 390519). **The Kings Head**, Llangennith, sells fabulous pies and traditional pub dishes; also offers accommodation (01792 386212; www.kingsheadgower.co.uk). **Maes-Yr-Haf**, Parkmill, is a chic restaurant with rooms that is just a short stroll away from Three Cliffs Bay (0845 085 0610; www.maes-yr-haf.com)

EXPLORE As Wild As You Want It is a great website with literally hundreds of links to companies that can arrange kayaking, coasteering, biking and sailing around the Gower Peninsula (www.aswildasyouwantit.com). **The Gower Way** is a 56.5-kilometre (35-mile) walking route around the peninsula; download routes (www.glamorgan walks.com)

TOURIST INFORMATION
www.visitswanseabay.com

GETTING THERE Nearest train station is Swansea (30.5 kilometres (19 miles) from Rhossili). **By road** follow the A4118, then take the B4247 to Rhossili

GOOD FOR Activity holidays, families, walkers, wildlife enthusiasts

there are dozens of different birds to spot and over 600 types of flowering plants to see. **Llangennith** is an atmospheric village right on the shore, nestling between the slopes of three hills, steeped in smugglers' tales and stories of shipwrecks.

For somewhere busier, a trip to the picturesque resort of **Mumbles** offers fantastic shopping in the boutiques and one-off shops on Newton Road that sell everything from couture to charcuterie. The resort also offers a glimpse of good old seaside kitsch on the Victorian pier. In the evening the 'Mumbles Mile' pub crawl provides a raucous night out. You'll be following in the footsteps of such illustrious drinkers as Dylan Thomas, who was a regular patron at **The Antelope** (01792 366835) on Mumbles Road.

OVERLEAF: Wooden ribs of the Helvetica *can been seen at low tide on Rhossili Bay.*

New Quay Ceredigion

Perched on the very tip of a headland on the west coast of Wales, overlooking the blue waters of Cardigan Bay, the small town of New Quay is steeped in history.

RIGHT: The picturesque harbour at New Quay.

Originally home to a motley mix of smugglers and fishermen, the town became a thriving boat-building centre. The narrow streets, rising in terraces, are linked by narrow passages that were once 'ropewalks', dating back to the town's shipbuilding heyday.

Nowadays, tourism is the main industry in **New Quay**. The town and surrounding area offer delightfully old-fashioned seaside pleasures – strolling along the quay with an ice cream or hot chips or rock-pooling for mussels, scallops and limpets. There is a clutch of dramatically beautiful beaches in the area: **Mwnt** – a wide stretch of sand protected by cliffs, with good parking – is ideal for families; **Cei Bach** is seldom busy, even though it's only 3 kilometres (2 miles) from New Quay.

One of the biggest draws is the dolphins. **Cardigan Bay** is probably the best place in Britain to see them and although boats run daily from the harbour with **New Quay Boat Trips** (www.newquayboattrips.co.uk), it's quite possible to simply stand on the quay and watch them glide through the water. The sea dominates life around New Quay. The boats tend to be pleasure cruisers now rather than fishing boats, although the waters still give up the freshest lobster and spider crabs that find their way into the restaurants in the town.

New Quay is also famous for its literary connections. Welsh poet Dylan Thomas began his most famous work, *Under Milk Wood*, while living here in the 1940s. There is a trail around the town and further afield that traces his life and the **New Quay Cliff Walk** was immortalized in his poem 'Quite Early One Morning'. The other unique walk near New Quay is through the heart of **Tregaron Bog**, which may sound a little unappealing but is actually a decked timber walkway across the rare raised peat bog. There are birdwatching hides and the

Penbryn is another unspoilt beach on Cardigan Bay.

area has a delightfully tranquil feel. (Maps are available from the Tourist Information Centre on Church Street.)

This corner of Wales is home to a clutch of picturesque former fishing villages, the prettiest of which is **Aberaeron**, an elegant Georgian town with a bustling harbour. One in four of the town's houses is listed, either because of historical or architectural interest. It's the perfect place to spend a morning gently pottering, before dropping into the **Clos Pencarreg Crafts Centre** (01545 570075).

The market town of **Cardigan** is also worth visiting, with 1,000 years of history and an attractive maze of winding streets lined with elegant Georgian and Victorian houses. The 19th-century market is a must-visit; go on a Thursday or Saturday when the Upper Hall is filled with a fantastic array of local produce along with jewellery, ceramics and clothes made by local craftspeople. Families should head to nearby **Cardigan Island Coastal Farm Park** (www.cardiganisland.co.uk), where seals, dolphins, wallabies and emus are all resident on the island, along with farm animals that children are welcome to feed.

RIGHT: Dolphins playing in Cardigan Bay.

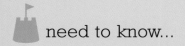

need to know...

ESSENTIAL · INFORMATION

SLEEP **Craig y Wig**, Glanmor Terrace, is a stylish bed and breakfast with a small front garden that's perfect for watching the dolphins frolicking in the bay (01545 561681; www.craig-y-wig.co.uk). **Cei Bach Country Club**, 2.5 kilometres (1½ miles) from New Quay, overlooks the beach at Cei Bach, with a restaurant and bar, kids' play area and nicely landscaped grounds (01454 580237; www.cei-bach.co.uk). **Harbourmaster Hotel**, Pen Cei, Aberaeron, has sleek rooms with roll-top baths and velvet sofas, and a renowned restaurant (01545 570755; www.harbour-master.com)

EAT **The Hungry Trout**, 2 South John Street, specializes in local seafood and has a great location right on the sea front. Also offers

accommodation (01545 560680, www.thehungrytrout.co.uk). **The Penwig**, South John Street, serves tasty gastropub dishes using local beef, lamb and fish, with indulgent home-made desserts. Accommodation also available (01545 560910; www.penwig.co.uk). **New Quay Honey Farm**, Cross Inn, a short trip out of town, is the perfect destination for those with a sweet tooth; it has a fabulous tea room (01545 560822; www.thehoneyfarm.co.uk)

EXPLORE **Dylan Thomas Trail** starts at the Tourist Information Centre down on the front (www.dylanthomaswales.org.uk). **Cilgerran Castle**, 5 kilometres (3 miles) south-east of Cardigan, is a striking 13th-century ruin that overlooks the Teifi Gorge (the company listed below offers guided canoeing trips through the gorge) (01443 336104; www.nationaltrust.org.uk). **Adventure Beyond** can organize canoeing trips, along with other activities including kayaking and coasteering (01239 851028; www.adventurebeyond.co.uk)

TOURIST INFORMATION **New Quay Tourist Information Centre**, Church Street (01545 580496). **www.newquay-westwales.co.uk**. **www.visitcardigan.com**

GETTING THERE **Nearest train station** is Aberystwyth (38 kilometres (23½ miles) from New Quay). **By road** New Quay is at the end of the A486, off the A487

GOOD FOR Activity holidays, families, walkers, wildlife enthusiasts

Isle of Wight

There is something deliciously old-fashioned about the Isle of Wight, as if somehow the Solent – the stretch of water that separates it from the south coast – has stopped the 21st century encroaching and kept it firmly in the realms of the 1970s.

RIGHT: The wild coast of the West Wight.

The pace of life is slower and towns have remained small and personal, with individual shops and cute cafés serving home-made cakes and ice-cream sundaes.

There are two very different sides to the island. The **East Wight** is home to the well-known resorts of **Shanklin**, **Sandown** and **Ventnor**, with their busy sandy beaches and traditional seaside feel. The **West Wight** is far wilder and more rural, criss-crossed by walking routes, scattered with country pubs and home to some of the island's most famous sites, from the **Needles**, that stretch out into the sea, to the vertiginous beach at **Alum Bay** with its famous coloured sands.

Family pleasures at Blackgang Chine.

Families are well catered for on the island. **Blackgang Chine** (www.blackgangchine.com) is an old-fashioned theme park that has entertained kids for decades, with roller coasters, water rides and rambling gardens full of fairy encampments and dinosaurs. For some serious dino-action, **Dinosaur Isle** (www.dinosaurisle.com) in Sandown is a must-visit, with an impressive collection of dinosaur fossils and lots of interactive exhibits. The old-fashioned rides at **Alum Bay** have been welcoming families for generations, along with the funicular ride down to the beach and the chance to fill glass bottles with the coloured sand.

Walking is the best way to discover the island and with 805 kilometres (500 miles) of trails (there are more walking routes than roads), there are routes for all levels of ability. The 108-kilometre (67-mile) **Isle of Wight Coastal Path** circumnavigates the island, with only gentle ascents and stunning views from some of the clifftop stretches. There are shorter inland trails, from 8–22.5 kilometres (5–14 miles), including the **Tennyson Way**, which takes in the monument on the top of

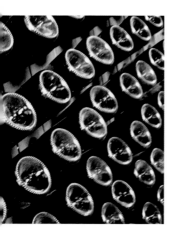

Vintages at Rosemary Vineyard.

View of Freshwater Bay by Tennyson Down.

Tennyson Down, dedicated to the famous poet who made the island his home.

Although the island is great for families and walkers it is also the perfect romantic escape. Over recent years there has been something of a foodie revolution on the island and there are smart hotels to stay in along with lots of cosy cottages. There are also several vineyards on the island that offer tastings and tours. **Rosemary Vineyard** (www.rosemaryvineyard.co.uk) near Ryde has 12 hectares (30 acres) of vines and has juices and ciders as well as wine to taste. Those with green fingers should head to the lush **Botanic Garden** (www. botanic.co.uk) at Ventnor, where the warm microclimate allows sub-tropical and exotic plants to bloom, alongside more familiar English country-garden flowers.

Sailors come for **Cowes Week** (www.cowesweek.co.uk), music lovers visit for the reborn **Isle of Wight Festival** (www.isleofwightfestival.com), walkers, foodies, parents bring their families back to the beaches they visited as children decades before – the island has wide appeal. Its magic is that somehow, in spite of welcoming hundreds of thousands of visitors each year, it manages to remain totally unspoilt.

need to know...

SLEEP **The Hambrough**, Hambrough Road, Ventnor, is the island's sleekest address. It has elegant bedrooms and a top-notch restaurant (01983 856333; www.thehambrough.com). **Carpenters Farm**, Carpenters Road, St Helens, has a campsite with plenty of space for children to play, along with an onsite shop and playground (01983 874557; www.carpentersfarm.co.uk). **St Catherine's Lighthouse**, just outside Niton, near Ventnor, makes for an unusual stay. There are three lighthouse-keepers' cottages to rent (01386 701177; www.ruralretreats.co.uk)

EAT **The New Inn**, Mill Road, Shalfleet, is one of the island's best gastropubs. It serves fresh fish and scrumptious puddings in a cosy, firelit interior (01983 531314; www.thenew-inn.co.uk). **Quay Arts Centre Café**, Sea Street, Newport Harbour, offers home-made lunches and cakes, with galleries to browse around before or afterwards (www.quayarts.org). **Steephill Cove Beach Café**, 1.5 kilometres (1 mile) west of Ventnor, can be reached by taking the clifftop walk from Ventnor to where the beachfront café serves locally caught crab (01983 855390; www. steephillcove.com)

EXPLORE **Wight Cycle Hire**, The Old Works, Station Road, Yarmouth, rents bikes and also runs weekly guided rides (01983 761800; www.wight cyclehire.co.uk). **Allendale Equestrian Centre**, Newport Road, Godshill, offers hacks and escorted rides for all abilities (01983 840258; www.allendale-ec.co.uk)

TOURIST INFORMATION
www.islandbreaks.co.uk

GETTING THERE **By ferry** – car and passenger ferries run from Portsmouth, Lymington and Southampton with **Wightlink** (0871 376 1000; www.wightlink.co.uk) and **Red Funnel** (0844 844 9988; www.redfunnel.co.uk)

GOOD FOR Couples, families, walkers

Brownsea Island and Studland Bay Dorset

The stunning natural harbour at Poole is the second largest in the world and combines busy tourist towns with Robinson Crusoe islands and glorious stretches of beach.

RIGHT: The rolling sand dunes of Shell Bay are at the very tip of the Studland Peninsula at the mouth of Poole Harbour.

The atmospheric ruins of Corfe Castle.

Brownsea Island is the biggest of the five islands in the harbour. Owned by the National Trust (www.nationaltrust.org.uk/Brownsea), it has an 81-hectare (200-acre) nature reserve that is home to a colony of rare red squirrels. However, it is probably most famous as the birthplace of the Scout and Guide movement, after Lord Baden-Powell tried the first experimental camp on the island in July 1907.

Although the island's campsite is only open to youth and school groups, there are plenty of ferries that ply the harbour's waters for day trips and the island is the perfect spot for a picnic and to watch the oystercatchers, kingfishers, terns and avocets that have made their home there. There is plenty to do on Brownsea, including open-air theatre productions, guided walks and activity weekends.

Across the water from Brownsea lies **Studland**, a small village that fronts on to a 5-kilometre (3-mile) stretch of unspoilt beach that is split into three picturesque sections, known as South, Middle and Knoll. Free from any development, the beaches are idyllic. They are backed by unspoilt heathland that teems with wildlife from nightjars and warblers to sand lizards and three types of snake. The nature reserve that spreads out from behind the beach feels wild and unspoilt; in the heart of it lies an area known as Little Sea, where the outside world is barely visible beyond the dunes.

The sheltered waters at Studland make it perfect for getting out on the water. There are dinghies and windsurfs to hire, and younger families can explore the coastline by pedalo or on banana and ringo rides (book through www.studlandwatersports.co.uk).

The village itself is part of the **Isle of Purbeck**, which stretches up to the pretty village of Swanage and the stunning ruins of Corfe Castle.

*Sunset over
Studland Bay.*

Although not strictly an island – it is only surrounded by the sea on three sides – it has retained a tranquil, unspoilt feel and it's hard to believe that the bright lights and bustle of Poole and Bournemouth are just 8 kilometres (5 miles) away. The quickest way to reach the towns is to hop on the ferry from Studland to **Sandbanks**. Known as Britain's Monte Carlo, it is well worth a stroll around just to see the gin palaces bobbing in the sunlight and the vast millionaires' mansions that sprawl down to the beach.

The combination of unspoilt beaches and bustling towns makes this a great destination for families with older children. Poole is home to **Splashdown** (www.splashdownpoole.co.uk), one of the biggest

*RIGHT: Family fun at
Studland.*

need to know...

ESSENTIAL • INFORMATION

SLEEP The Knoll House, Studland Bay, is a family-friendly hotel with an adventure playground, pool and spa (01929 450450; www.knollhouse. co.uk). **Burnbake Campsite**, Rempstone, is a secluded site between Corfe Castle and Studland. Set in 5 hectares (12 acres) of woodland, it has a well-stocked shop and good facilities (01929 480570; www.btinternet.com/~burnbakecampsite). **Bankes Arms Country Inn**, Manor Road, Studland, combines a microbrewery with hearty pub meals and comfortable bedrooms (01929 450255; www.bankesarms.com)

EAT Shell Bay Seafood Restaurant and Bar, Ferry Road, Studland, has an idyllic location right on the waterfront and serves up locally caught fish and seafood (01929 450363; www.shellbay. net). **The Blue Pool Tea Rooms**, just north of the Purbeck Hills in Furzebrook, serves home-made cakes and traditional lunches overlooking a beautiful lake (01929 551408; www.bluepool tearooms.co.uk). **TJ's Fish and Chips**, Sandbanks Road, Lilliput – the best place to eat is on the

beach itself, so pick up fish and chips from this shop, which offers exotic catch such as barramundi, sea bass and calamari (01202 707691)

EXPLORE Poole Harbour Trails is a newly created series of walking and cycling trails, with start and finish points at bus stops (www.pooleharbourtrails.org.uk). **Studland Stables**, Ferry Road, Studland, can arrange rides so that you can explore the area on horseback (01929 450273; www.studlandstables.com)

TOURIST INFORMATION www.iknow-dorset.co.uk

GETTING THERE By ferry – services from Poole Quay and Sandbanks with **Greenslades** (01202 631828; www.greensladepleasureboats.co.uk) or **Brownsea Island Ferries** (01929 462383; www.brownseaislandferries.com)

GOOD FOR Activity holidays, families, wildlife enthusiasts

waterparks in the UK, while **Oceanarium** in Bournemouth (www.oceanarium.co.uk) is a spectacular aquarium offering eight different underwater regions to explore, from the Mediterranean to the Antarctic ice shelf. **Poole Quay** is a great spot to stop for lunch, with the harbour-front restaurants offering front-row seats for watching the endless parade of boats, pleasure-cruisers, ferries and yachts sailing out into the blue waters of the English Channel.

Lulworth Cove and Durdle Door Dorset

The perfect arc of sand at Lulworth Cove and the giant limestone arch of
Durdle Door are two of the most iconic images of the British coastline.

*RIGHT: Stately Lulworth
Castle.*

Surrounded by the dramatic cliffs that dominate Dorset's slice of the
Jurassic Coast, the golden beaches teem with visitors in the summer
but out of season it's possible to have these stunning stretches of
shoreline almost to yourself.

*The picturesque cove of
Lulworth.*

The best way to discover them both is to follow the well-trodden path
that leads west from Lulworth Cove, up and over the cliffs to Durdle
Door. From the top it's possible to see the perfect horseshoe shape of

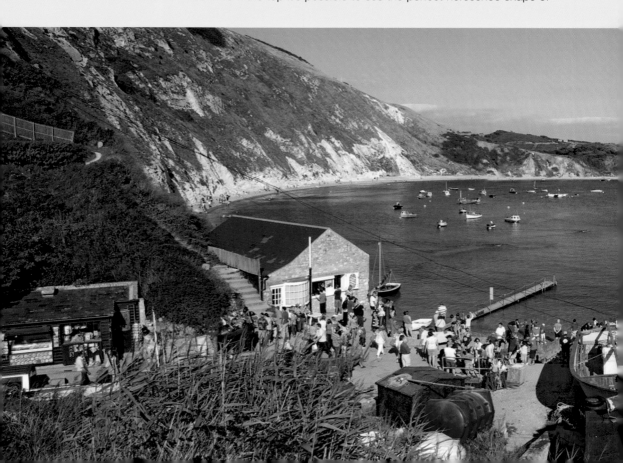

Lulworth, created over thousands of years by the sea eroding the softer rock that exists behind the hard Portland stone entrance to the cove. The dramatic Durdle Door has been similarly created by the sea wearing away the weaker rock, leaving a natural archway above the sea. Head east from Lulworth Cove and there is a stunning clifftop walk through a fossilized forest and down to the sea at **Mupe Bay**. The footpath does run through Ministry of Defence land, however, and is only open at weekends and throughout August.

The two parts of **Lulworth** village – east and west – lie about 800 metres (½ mile) behind the beach. Both are picturebook pretty, with thatched cottages and a village pub, although **East Lulworth** is

Evening over Durdle Door.

dominated by the sprawling **Lulworth Estate** (www.lulworth.com), which is home to an impressive castle that dates back to the mid-17th century. Restored in the mid-1990s after a major fire had left it derelict for decades, it is open to the public, along with a children's animal farm, a café, shop and glorious parkland, perfect for a picnic.

There's plenty to discover on **Lulworth Cove** itself; as with much of the Jurassic Coast there are fossils to search for and you can find plenty of information on the unique geology of the region at the **Lulworth Cove Heritage Centre** (www.lulworth.com), which is free to enter. This stretch of coastline is studded with picturesque beaches and coves. Nearby **Kimmeridge** offers fabulous rock-pooling possibilities at low tide, when long, rocky ledges that are home to crabs, fish and anemones protrude from the water. The seas also offer excellent snorkelling; at Kimmeridge

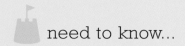

need to know...

ESSENTIAL • INFORMATION

SLEEP **The Beach House**, Lulworth Cove, West Lulworth, has 11 sleek rooms and a restaurant serving up local seafood (01929 400404; www.lulworthbeachhotel.com). **Durdle Door Holiday Park**, signposted from West Lulworth village, is part of the Lulworth Estate and includes two camping areas with excellent facilities (01929 400200; www.lulworth.com). **The Stone Barn**, Kimmeridge, is a luxury self-catering barn conversion, sleeping 10, perfect for a house party or family gathering (0800 9804070; www.dorset coastalcottages.com)

EAT **The Castle Inn**, Main Road, West Lulworth, serves classic pub grub in a pretty 16th-century thatched building (01929 400311; www.thecastleinn-lulworthcove.co.uk). **Finley's**, Main Road, West Lulworth gives you the chance to experience the best of both worlds: pop in for fish and chips and take them down to munch on the beach as the sun sets (01929 400711). **Crab House Café**, Ferrymans Way, Wyke Regis, has views over the coast and offers fantastic oysters (01305 788867; www.crabhousecafe.co.uk)

EXPLORE **Lulworth Heritage Centre** has information about the surrounding area and can arrange guided excursions (01929 400587; www.lulworth.com)

TOURIST INFORMATION **www.purbeck-dc.gov.uk/purbeck_tourism.aspx**

GETTING THERE **Nearest train station** is Wareham (9.5 kilometres (6 miles) from East Lulworth, 13.5 kilometres (8½ miles) from West Lulworth). **By road** East and West Lulworth are on the B3070, accessible from the A352

GOOD FOR Couples, families, walkers

there is a snorkelling trail marked by buoys in the water, while **Bowleaze Cove** near **Weymouth** teems with bass, wrasse and pipefish.

The area surrounding Lulworth is steeped in history. The spectacular ruins of **Corfe Castle** (www.nationaltrust.org.uk) are just 16 kilometres (10 miles) away, offering lots of scrambling and climbing potential for kids and a fascinating insight into 1,000 years of history for adults. One of the best ways to get an overview of the surrounding area is on the **Swanage Heritage Railway** (www.swanagerailway.co.uk), which runs heritage steam and diesel trains through 9.5 kilometres (6 miles) of Dorset countryside. But the most spectacular countryside is the coast itself; 150 million years of history visible in the spectacular cliff faces, all linked together by the **South West Coast Path** (www.southwest coastpath.com).

Lyme Regis and Charmouth Dorset

Dorset's Jurassic Coast is one of the most spectacular stretches of shoreline in Britain: towering cliffs, sandy beaches littered with fossils and atmospheric small towns that offer refreshingly old-fashioned seaside holidays.

RIGHT: *The fishing harbour at Lyme Regis.*

Lyme Regis and **Charmouth** complement each other perfectly; the busy beaches and picturesque streets of Lyme provide a contrast to the quieter, sleepy feel of Charmouth. Both share the spectacular coastline, where blissfully peaceful afternoons can be spent on the gently shelving beaches, swimming, crabbing or hunting for fossils.

Lyme Regis, the more famous of the two, is best known for the **Cobb** – the long stone breakwater that stretches out into the sea, creating the town's harbour. A windswept walk along it – following in the footsteps of Meryl Streep in *The French Lieutenant's Woman* – is an essential part of a visit to Lyme, along with the climb up to **Timber Hill** for the panoramic views over the rooftops. The town is a clutter of steep narrow streets lined with tea rooms and galleries – the Blue Lias Gallery (www.bluelias. co.uk) on Coombe Street is one of the best.

Lyme may be well known but one of its greatest treasures is hidden away from the tourist hordes. The **Undercliff** (www.jurassiccoast.com) is one of the last wilderness areas of the UK, a nature reserve formed from landslides that have happened over centuries. The reserve is home to a spectacular mix of plants and wildlife and there is a clearly marked route through the reserve, part of the **South West Coast Path** (www.southwestcoastpath.com).

Charmouth is smaller and quieter, its beach dominated by the towering face of **Golden Cap**, the highest point in southern England. From the car park at **Stonebarrow Hill** at the southern end of the village, the walk to the top and back is around 8 kilometres (5 miles). It's a pull up to the peak of 191 metres (626½ feet) but the stunning views make it worth the effort. On the walk back it's worth diverting to the seaside village of **Seatown** for a restorative drink at the beachfront **The Anchor Inn** pub (01297 489215).

need to know...

bedrooms and an eclectic restaurant (01308 868358; www.theshavecrossinn.co.uk). **Wood Farm Caravan and Camping Park**, western side of Charmouth, is a well-established and beautifully kept site (01297 560697; www.woodfarm.co.uk)

EAT **Georgian Tea Rooms**, 53 Broad Street, Lyme Regis, does the best clotted cream tea in town (01297 442961). **Hix Oyster & Fish House**, Cobb Road, Lyme Regis, is in a spectacular location overlooking the Cobb. It offers the pick of the day's catch from the town's fishing fleet (01297 446910; www.hixoysterandfishhouse.co.uk). **The Royal Oak**, The Street, Charmouth, serves good pub food sourced from local producers (01297 560277; www.royaloakcharmouth.co.uk)

EXPLORE **Joint Venture** will take you out fishing and on sightseeing boat tours from Lyme Regis (01297 442656). **Lyme Regis Fossil Walks** offers guided walks along the coast (07854 377519; www.lymeregisfossilwalks.com). There are **guided walks** over Golden Cap and around the area; details from Lyme Regis Tourist Information Centre

TOURIST INFORMATION **Lyme Regis Tourist Information Centre**, Guildhall Cottage, Church Street (01297 442138; www.lyme-regis-dorset. co.uk). **www.westdorset.com**

GETTING THERE **Nearest train station** is Axminster (9 kilometres (5½ miles) from Lyme Regis and 10.5 kilometres (6½ miles) from Charmouth). **By road** the A35 runs through Charmouth, turn off on to the A3052 to reach Lyme Regis

GOOD FOR Families, walkers, wildlife enthusiasts

SLEEP **Alexandra Hotel and Restaurant**, Pound Street, Lyme Regis, is sleekly elegant, welcoming to families and has top-notch food (01297 442010; www.hotelalexandra.co.uk). **The Shave Cross Inn**, Shave Cross, Bridport, has luxurious four-poster

In the surrounding area there's plenty to explore. The town of **Bridport** has an excellent market on Wednesdays and Saturdays, when local farmers bring meats, cheeses and vegetables straight from the surrounding fields. Kids will adore the **Wildlife Park at Cricket St Thomas** (www.wild.org.uk), which boasts leopards, cheetahs and camels among its residents, while for garden lovers, **Montacute House** (www.nationaltrust.org.uk) is a great choice for a tranquil day out, with vibrant, flower-filled borders dotting the 121.5 hectares (300 acres) of grounds.

But it's the coastline that really has the wow factor. Dating back over 180 million years, the **Jurassic Coast** is England's first natural UNESCO World Heritage Site and the dramatic cliffs and sweeping beaches are best seen from the sea. Trips run from Lyme Regis on most days. Pick up a tub of clotted cream and some fresh scones from **Town Mill Bakery** on Coombe Street (01297 444035) and have yourself a West Country picnic on the water or book a fishing trip and bring home fresh mackerel for supper.

LEFT: A solitary rider on Lyme Bay.

Atmospheric Seaton Hole is a short distance west along the Jurassic Coast, just across the county border in Devon.

Rye East Sussex

The steep cobbled streets, individual shops and boutiques, and medieval houses make Rye one of the most atmospheric and delightful of all Britain's seaside towns.

RIGHT: Rye's windmill.

Camber Castle is part of Rye Harbour Nature Reserve.

One of the Cinque Ports – an ancient collection of coastal towns that formed a defensive and trading group – it has a unique status as it is no longer actually on the sea. Originally built on an outcrop of rock as an important defensive position, the sea retreated in the 16th century, leaving the town to look out over the River Rother and Romney Marshes to the English Channel beyond.

Rye is the kind of town that could only exist in England: quirky, traditional, heaving with charm. The best way to get to know the town is

to wander along the streets. Don't miss **Mermaid Street** and **West Street**, lined with ancient houses, and **Conduit Hill**, where the former Augustinian priory now houses a working pottery. Rye is home to a number of craftsmen and artists and is particularly famous for its pottery, which has been made in the town since the 11th century. Visit Rye Art Gallery (www.ryeartgallery.co.uk) on the High Street to browse the watercolours, oil paintings and sculpture.

The town's most famous landmark is the **Ypres Tower**, which dates back to 1250 and is the oldest building in Rye open to the public. Originally built as part of the town's defences, it's now part of the **Rye Castle Museum** (www.ryemuseum.co.uk). The Ypres Tower site is dedicated to the town's fascinating history and along with the exhibits it offers stunning views across the rooftops from the tower's balcony.

The town also makes a perfect base for exploring the surrounding countryside. The beaches at **Camber** and **Winchelsea** are ideal for swimming, while **Bedgebury Pinetum** (www.bedgeburypinetum.org.uk) offers cycling and walking trails and activity areas for kids. The stunning castle at **Bodiam** (www.nationaltrust.org.uk) is a short drive away. Dating back to medieval times and surrounded by a moat, it has a true fairytale feel and kids can even try on armour.

Walkers are well catered for, with an easy footpath across the marshes to **Camber Castle**, built by Henry VIII in the 16th century to protect Rye from invasion. The **Royal Military Canal** (www.royalmilitarycanal.com) is excellent to walk beside, with plenty of wildlife-spotting potential, while **Rye Harbour Nature Reserve** (www.wildrye.info) is famous for its rich birdlife and is criss-crossed with footpaths.

But the greatest pleasure to be had in Rye is simply strolling around the streets, soaking up the atmosphere and stopping for coffee at one of the numerous cafés. There are famous footsteps to follow: Henry James lived in the town for 18 years and Spike Milligan spent the last years of his life in Rye. James's home, **Lamb House** on West Street, is open to the public (www.nationaltrust.org.uk), while **The Gandhi Tandoori** (01797 223091), Milligan's curry house of choice, is still serving up top-notch food.

Part of Rye Harbour Nature Reserve, the Beach Reserve is a large expanse of bare shingle ridges.

need to know...

SLEEP **The George in Rye**, 98 High Street, is a classically elegant hotel, with individually designed rooms and a renowned restaurant (01797 222114; www.thegeorgeinrye.com). **The Apothecary**, 1 East Street, provides a new spin on a bed and breakfast, offering elegant, centrally located rooms above a coffee shop, where breakfast is served (01797 229157). **The Mermaid Inn**, Mermaid Street, dates back to the 15th century and offers classic English style (01797 223065; www.mermaid inn.com)

EAT **Webbe's at the Fish Café**, 17 Tower Street, is the place for fish and fantastic seafood platters (01797 222226; www.thefishcafe.com). **The Ship Inn**, The Strand, does top-notch pub food, all locally sourced, (01797 222233; www.theshipinn rye.co.uk). **Fletcher's House**, 2 Lion Street, is one of Rye's oldest tea rooms. It has a charming walled garden and is definitely the place for afternoon tea (01797 222227; www.fletchershouse.co.uk)

EXPLORE **Rye Hire**, 1 Cyprus Place, rents bicycles. Head off along the Tour de la Manche cycle trail or down to the nature reserve at Rye Harbour (01797 223033). **Romney, Hythe and Dymchurch Railway** operates miniature trains that runs from Hythe to Dungeness (01797 362353; www.rhdr.org.uk). **Kent and East Sussex Railway** runs full-size restored steam trains from Tenterden to Bodiam; this is a fantastic way to see the surrounding countryside. There are Santa Specials trains on certain days in December (01580 765155 (general enquires) 01580 762943 (24-hour talking timetable); www.kesr.org.uk)

TOURIST INFORMATION **www.visitrye.co.uk**

GETTING THERE **Nearest train station** is Rye. **By road** the A259 runs through the town

GOOD FOR Couples, families, walkers, wildlife enthusiasts

Whitstable Kent

Whitstable is a unique mix of gentrification and good, old-fashioned seaside charm. It has a charmingly rundown High Street leading to a beach dotted with elegant seafood restaurants. Its history is entwined with the sea.

RIGHT: The unspoilt beach at the Seasalter end of West Beach.

During the Napoleonic Wars it was rife with smuggling and the town is still criss-crossed with eccentrically named alleyways such as **Squeeze Gut Alley** and **Collar's Alley**, which were originally planned to give residents increased access to the sea but were more often used as convenient escape routes for law-breakers.

If you come to Whitstable expecting the polish of somewhere like Padstow (Cornwall) then you may be a little disappointed. The town has a far more rakish charm, in keeping with its slightly disreputable past, and there is a mix of art galleries, such as the **Walker-Platt Gallery** on Oxford Street (www.thewalkerplattgallery.com), and simple cafés and everyday shops. The best place for a stroll and shopping is along **Harbour Street**, where a jumble of cottages and houses are now home to individual boutiques. Dip into **Mosaic** (01227 276779) for Fairtrade and ethnic jewellery, ceramics and gifts from around the world or take the kids into Buttercup (01227 265978), which sells beautiful wooden children's toys and is owned by children's author Emma Thomson.

Whitstable's working fishing harbour.

But where the kids will really want to be is on the beach and Whitstable has a number of different stretches, meaning that there's always plenty of room to spread out. The beaches aren't sandy but the sea is usually calm and excellent for swimming. For lunch on the pebbles head to **The Old Neptune** pub (www.neppy.co.uk), which sits right on the **West Beach**, or take a picnic over to **Tankerton Slopes**, a wide stretch of beach that separates Whitstable from neighbouring Tankerton. There are two good coastal walks from the town's beaches along the waymarked **Saxon Shore Way**: a 6.5-kilometre (4-mile) walk to neighbouring **Herne Bay**, following long beach-side promenades or a

*Whitstable beach
at sunset.*

longer 16-kilometre (10-mile) walk to **Faversham**, past streams edged
with bulrushes that offer fantastic birdwatching potential.

Foodies are well catered for in town, with plenty of restaurants
making the most of the local fishermen's daily haul. It's worth strolling
down to the **harbour fish market**, where piles of fresh fish and huge
catches of crabs and seafood are laid out for locals, restaurateurs and
visitors to buy.

There's plenty to explore within a short drive of the town. One must-
visit is the city of **Canterbury**, roughly half an hour's drive away and
home to the most beautiful cathedral in the whole of Britain. Try and visit
mid-afternoon when you can sit and listen to evensong. Take a walk
around the back of the cathedral through the tranquil precincts that lead
to the Kings School, which has been in operation since 1597.

Whether you visit Whitstable in summer, when the beaches are
scattered with families and the restaurant terraces are spilling over with
customers or in the winter, when the windswept beaches and clear blue
skies have a very tranquil beauty, you're just as likely to fall prey to its
charms. Whitstable really is a town for all seasons.

*RIGHT: Discover local
artists in Whitstable.*

SLEEP **Converted fisherman's hut** right on the beach is the most authentic place to stay. The huts sleep between two and four (01227 280280; www.hotelcontinental.co.uk). **Harbour Cottage**, Bexley Street, is just one street back from the sea; an elegantly restored self-catering house that sleeps four (07799 413975). **Hotel Continental**, 29 Beach Walk, is the best non-self-catering option (contact details as above)

EAT **The Crab & Winkle Fish & Seafood Restaurant**, South Quay – follow your nose to this restaurant for fabulous seafood platters with sea views to match (0845 2571587; www.seafood-restaurant-uk.com/). **Wheelers Oyster Bar**, 8 High Street, is simpler but has equally fresh fish. It's a tiny place that has been serving up the day's catch for more than 150 years (01227 273311). **Williams and Brown Tapas Bar**, 48 Harbour Street, is the place to go if you're all fished out or pack up a picnic using produce from their deli a few doors along (01227 273373; www.thetapas.co.uk)

EXPLORE **Crab and Winkle Way** is an 11.5-kilometre (7-mile) cycle route that follows part of the old Canterbury and Whitstable railway line (www.crabandwinkle.org). **Greta Thames Sailing Barge** offers you the chance to enjoy a sedate day sailing from Whitstable Harbour around the Thames Estuary (07711 657919; www.greta 1892.co.uk)

TOURIST INFORMATION
www.canterbury.co.uk

GETTING THERE **Nearest train station** is Whitstable. **By road** Whitstable is on the B2205, off the A2990

GOOD FOR Couples, families

Brighton East Sussex

In the past few years Brighton has undergone a spectacular reinvention. The drab three-star hotels and scrappy seafront have been replaced by sleek boutique hotels, hip restaurants and a bohemian atmosphere that has lured in celebrities and seen the town's profile go through the roof.

RIGHT: Traditional seaside pleasures on the pier.

The gleaming spires of the Pavilion.

It's still a town of two halves: the modern western half of the town has a huge shopping centre and chain restaurants, while the east is home to the famous Lanes and the trendy quarters of **Kemp Town** and North Laine.

Sooner or later, everyone in Brighton ends up on the **beach**. It is pebbly, dominated by its pier and always busy but there is a great selection of bars and restaurants in the archways and promenades that front on to the shore. For quieter lazing its better to stroll away from town, either west to **Hove** or east past the marina, although bear in mind that a long section of this area is a nudist beach.

Just back from the beach lie the **Lanes**; a picturesque clutter of tiny alleyways that date back to when Brighton was a small fishing village, originally lined with terraced cottages and flint fishermen's houses. Now these buildings hold designer boutiques, jewellery and antique shops, juice bars and brasseries and it's easy to spend a whole day lost in the atmospheric maze of streets. If the tourist crowds get overwhelming, head up to **North Laine** (www.northlaine.co.uk), a collection of six small streets that are home to a fantastic mix of ethnic shops and cafés. On Saturdays there is an atmospheric flea market and some of the streets are closed to traffic, giving the area an open-air, almost Mediterranean feel.

Between the two sets of lanes lies the **Royal Pavilion** (www.royalpavilion.org.uk), a stunning oriental building studded with domes and minarets, which took 35 years to build under the eccentric direction of George IV. Inside, the building is equally opulent. Gilded dragons, carved palm trees and imitation bamboo staircases all create an exotic feel that is a world away from the more formal atmosphere that usually defines royal residences.

EAT Due South, 139 Kings Road Arches, is an elegant eatery right on the beach that sources all its food from within 56.5 kilometres (35 miles) of Brighton; expect local shellfish, lamb and cheeses (01273 821218; www.duesouth.co.uk). **Terre à Terre**, 71 East Street, is an award-winning veggie restaurant in the South Lanes (01273 729051; www.terreaterre.co.uk). **Tea Cosy**, 3 George Street, is the place for tea lovers but be warned, biscuit dunking is not allowed! (01273 267929; www.theteacosy.co.uk)

EXPLORE Cool City Walks offers downloadable audio walking tours and guides to the city (0844 4871052; www.coolcitywalks.com). **The South Downs Way** skirts the hills just beyond Brighton, including Ditchling Beacon (01243 558716; www.nationaltrail.co.uk/southdowns/). **Breeze buses** run from the town centre to the South Downs (01273 822073; www.buses.co.uk)

TOURIST INFORMATION
www.visitbrighton.com

GETTING THERE Nearest train station is Brighton. **By road** the A23 runs south from the M25 into Brighton town centre

GOOD FOR Couples, families

SLEEP Drakes, 43–44 Marine Parade, is the perfect choice for a naughty weekend away. It is an elegant townhouse hotel right on the seafront with sleek rooms and a top-notch restaurant (01273 696934; www.drakesofbrighton.com). **One Broad Street** is a chic bed and breakfast in the trendy Kemp Town area and has stylish white bedrooms and a sunny breakfast room (01273 699227; www.onebroadstreet.com). **The Grand**, 97–99 King's Road, is the place to stay if budget is not an issue and your taste is old-school glamour. Plush bedrooms overlook the sea and cocktails and afternoon tea are de rigueur (0845 3752808 (reservations); www.devere.co.uk/our-locations/the-grand.html)

Brighton is perfectly placed to explore the glorious surrounding countryside. Ten minutes' drive out of town and you are on the top of the **South Downs** (www.visitsouthdowns.com). **Devils Dyke** is a dramatic V-shaped valley that offers fabulous walking, while the village of **Ditchling** has a delightfully rural feel. The village is in the shadow of the National Trust-owned Ditchling Beacon (www.nationaltrust.org.uk), which is another great spot for a walk. The pretty village of **Rottingdean** is a short drive away and has its own stretch of beach.

If the British weather does its worst there are plenty of indoor attractions. Kids will love the **Sea Life** centre (www.sealife.co.uk), which is the oldest operating aquarium in the world, while couples can curl up in front of a vintage movie at the **Duke of York's Picturehouse** (www.picturehouses.co.uk), Preston Circus, Britain's oldest cinema.

However, whether rain or shine, the best way to get to know Brighton is to walk – between the countless bars, boutiques and brasseries and, of course, the beach.

LEFT: Brighton's colourful, annual festival.

The tranquil beauty of the South Downs.

Blackpool Sands Devon

There's a Mediterranean feel to this pine-fringed, sheltered, shingle beach near the bustling port of Dartmouth, particularly when the sun is out and the water is a deep turquoise green.

RIGHT: Thurlestone Rock near Salcombe in the South Hams.

The idyllic landscape of Blackpool Sands.

Boasting a Blue Flag award for its clean and safe bathing and excellent facilities, family-friendly **Blackpool Sands** (www.blackpool sands.co.uk) is the perfect base for a bucket-and-spade holiday. There are sandpits for kids (May to end of peak season), summer lifeguards, a freshwater paddling pool, showers and even a lost-child collection point.

Superb watersport facilities also make it popular with older children and adults. Hire a windsurf or kayak from the Royal Yacht Association-recognized training centre, **Lushwind** (www.lushwind.co.uk), next to the beach café or book one of their courses (children over eight), which run from May to late October. You can also try paddleboarding, where you stand up on a surfboard and use a long paddle; it's hard work but great exercise.

One of Blackpool Sands' biggest draws is the award-winning **Venus Beach Café** (www.venuscompany.co.uk/bPoolsands.php), which uses local, organic produce. It's open every day of the year except Christmas Day. Start the day with a full West Country breakfast, lunch on a free-

range chicken Caesar salad with a glass of chilled, local Sharpham wine and finish the day with Start Bay grilled lobster from the barbecue. Kids' food is suitably wholesome, including organic pasta with tomato and basil sauce, and kids get an activity book to distract them while you eat your meal. There's also a shop selling beach paraphernalia and local produce.

Drive – or take a bus – west towards Start Point and you'll come to the spectacular **Slapton Sands**, a 5-kilometre (3-mile) long stretch of fine shingle beach backed by a freshwater lake and **Slapton Ley**, an internationally renowned nature reserve. It was on Slapton Sands that the Americans practised the D-Day landings, which ended in tragedy when more than 1,000 Allied troops were attacked by German boats. A Sherman tank recovered from the sea is now a memorial to those who died. It is at the southern end of the beach at Torcross.

The **South Hams** has plenty of lush tropical gardens to visit; the nearest to Blackpool Sands is just through a little green door at the back of the beach, opposite the entrance. Climb to the top for spectacular views across **Start Bay**.

Two National Trust gardens (www.nationaltrust.org.uk), **Coleton Fishacre**, a luxuriant oasis with an arts and crafts-style house overlooking the sea at Kingswear and Agatha Christie's summer retreat **Greenway** on the banks of the River Dart, can be reached by ferry from Dartmouth Quay.

If you fancy a bit of history head to the 600-year-old **Dartmouth Castle** (www.english-heritage.org.uk), guarding the entrance to the narrow Dart Estuary and open year-round.

On the other side of the river, reached on foot or by car ferry, is **Kingswear**, with its pretty pastel-coloured houses and terminus for the **Paignton Steam Railway** (www.pdsr.co.uk). The railway runs alongside the River Dart and the Torbay coastline to Paignton. **Totnes**, with its plethora of New Age shops and vegetarian cafés, is also a boat ride upstream. But if that all sounds too much like hard work, browse around the boutiques and galleries in **Dartmouth** – or go crabbing on the quay – before enjoying a fresh fish supper in one of the town's restaurants.

Kayaking is a popular sport on Blackpool Sands.

RIGHT: Dartmouth is a pleasant place to wander around.

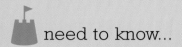

ESSENTIAL · INFORMATION

SLEEP Kingswear Castle, on the east shore of the Dart Estuary, is available to rent. Sleeps four (01628 825925; www.landmarktrust.co.uk). **Leonards Cove**, Stoke Fleming, is a campsite, caravan park and has self-catering cottages with sea views (01803 770206; www.leonardscoveholidaycamping.co.uk). **StaysAfloat**, Dartmouth Marina, offers moored luxury yachts sleeping up to six (01803 833810; www.staysafloat.com).

EAT The Brill Plaice, situated within Leonards Cove, Stoke Fleming (see above), is a contemporary bistro that serves fresh fish and has great sea views (www.brill-plaice.co.uk). **The**

Green Dragon, Church Street, Stoke Fleming, has wood beams, stone floors and an open fire. Serves fresh fish, vegetarian dishes and local beer (01803 770238; www.green-dragon-pub.co.uk). **The New Angel**, 2 South Embankment, Dartmouth, is celebrity chef John Burton Race's Michelin-starred restaurant overlooking the River Dart. It offers fresh and seasonal produce cooked in a French style (01803 839425; www.theangel.co.uk)

EXPLORE Treasure Trails offers a murder mystery trail around Dartmouth; download the trail then solve the clues (while exploring Dartmouth) to find out whodunnit (01726 68829; www.treasure trails.co.uk). **Falcon of Dartmouth Boat Charters** offers boat trips from Dartmouth on the *Falcon* with owner/skipper Tony Hoile, who specializes in watching seabirds, seals, peregrine falcons and has also spotted basking sharks, dolphins and turtles (01803 839245; www.dartboat.com). **Start Point Lighthouse**, south side of Start Bay, is open for tours on selected dates between February and October (020 7481 6900; www.trinityhouse.co.uk)

TOURIST INFORMATION Dartmouth Tourist Information Centre, The Engine House, Mayors Avenue (01803 834224; www.discover dartmouth.com). **www.visitsouthdevon.co.uk**

GETTING THERE Nearest train station is Totnes (25.5 kilometres (16 miles) from Blackpool Sands). **By road** follow the A379 from Dartmouth, located between Stoke Fleming and Strete

GOOD FOR Activity holidays, couples, families, walkers, wildlife enthusiasts

Branscombe Devon

You have to drive along a long, narrow, winding lane with steep-sided valleys to reach one of East Devon's most picturesque villages, with its chocolate-box thatched cottages and two atmospheric 14th-century pubs.

Branscombe is renowned for its thatched cottages and Devonshire cream teas.

RIGHT: Walkers on the coastal hills near Branscombe.

Branscombe Mouth, a National Trust-run (www.nationaltrust.org.uk) shingle beach, whose water turns an enticing turquoise colour in the summer, offers great swimming and stone-skimming opportunities. The thatched **Sea Shanty Restaurant and Shop** (www.theseashanty .co.uk), directly behind, is big on local seafood including Lyme Bay Crab, landed by fisherman John Hughes on the beach.

Locally caught lobster and crab is also featured on the menu of the 14th-century **The Mason's Arms** (www.masonsarms.co.uk). With fireplaces, slate floors and exposed stone walls, the pub is a cosy place for a fireside drink on a chilly day. You'll find locals playing dominoes and dogs stretched out under tables. In summer there's a beer festival, when you can sample local bitters including those from the village's own **Branscombe Vale Brewery** (01297 680511).

There are excellent walks along the **South West Coast Path** (www.southwestcoastpath.com) in both directions. Head east, along a fine stretch of chalk cliff interspersed by landslips and noted for fossils – the village is on the **Jurassic Coast** – to the old fishing and smuggling village of **Beer**. Here you can pick up some fresh sole or flounder from the fisherman's hut above the beach. Beer is also famous for its lace making; Queen Victoria's wedding dress was made here.

Visit the awe-inspring **Beer Quarry Caves** (www.beerquarrycaves .com), open from March to October, which looks like an underground cathedral, and once provided a refuge for persecuted Catholics as well being used as a store for smugglers' contraband. Many of Branscombe's cottages were made with Beer stone, also used to build Exeter Cathedral, Westminster Abbey and Windsor Castle.

Step 300 years back in time to Branscombe's National Trust-restored **Old Bakery, Manor Mill and Forge** (www.nationaltrust.org.uk), which is still in full working order. Watch the traditional handcraft of ironwork in the only working thatched forge left in the country before enjoying a superb Devon cream tea in the thatched Old Bakery, with its old-fashioned baking equipment and open fires.

A short walk out of Branscombe takes you to the **Donkey Sanctuary** (www.thedonkeysanctuary.org.uk), a free, charity-run attraction open year-round. You can wander around the fields making a fuss of the 500 or so donkeys and enjoy the picturesque views or have lunch or a cream tea in the rustic Hayloft Restaurant.

Kids – and big kids – will love riding on the open-top narrow gauge heritage trams (www.tram.co.uk). They run from the nearby resort of **Seaton** along the lush **Axe Valley**, famous for its wading birds, to the pretty village of **Colyton,** with its sumptuous church and village square. Trams operate mostly from April to October and on selected dates throughout the rest of the year (except January). **Crealy Adventure Park** (www.crealy.co.uk) near Exeter, open all year, is also a great day out for kids. There are animals to cuddle, plenty of fun rides and indoor play areas.

RIGHT: Signposts on the South West Coast Path near Branscombe.

FAR RIGHT: The only working thatched forge in the country at Branscombe.

BELOW: The chocolate-box thatched cottages in Branscombe.

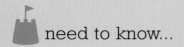

need to know...

ESSENTIAL • INFORMATION

SLEEP The Mason's Arms has 18 en suite rooms, some with sea and valley views and four-poster beds (01297 680300; www.masons arms.co.uk). **Coombe View Farm** is a stunning rural campfire-permitting campsite on the edge of the village (01297 680218; www.coombe view.fsnet.co.uk). **Thatched Clematis Cottage** has wooden beams, a wood-burning stove, two double bedrooms and is next door to The Fountain Head pub (see below) (01342 851155; www.devon hols.co.uk)

EAT The Mason's Arms specializes in meat roasted over an open fire (see above). **The Fountain Head** has slate floors, an open fire and holds spit roasts. There is live music every Sunday during the summer (01297 680359; www.fountain headinn.com). **The Old Bakery**, run by The National Trust, makes excellent cream teas (01752 346585; www.nationaltrust.org.uk)

EXPLORE John Hughes, a local skipper, offers sea-fishing trips from Branscombe beach (01297

680369). **Stuart Line Cruises** runs open-topped boat trips from Exmouth along the Jurassic Coast or up the River Exe to Topsham (summer – 01395 222144; winter – 01395 279693; www.stuartline cruises.co.uk). **Bicton Park Botanical Gardens**, East Budleigh, is an 18th-century landscaped park set in the pretty Otter Valley, with kids' indoor and outdoor play areas, Italian garden and a stunning 1820s curvilinear glass house. Open all year (01395 568465; www.bictongardens.co.uk)

TOURIST INFORMATION Seaton Tourist Information Centre, The Underfleet, Harbour Road (01297 21660; www.seatontic.com). **www.visitdevon.co.uk**

GETTING THERE Nearest train station is Honiton (19.5 kilometres (12 miles) from Branscombe). **By road** Branscombe is off the A3052

GOOD FOR Couples, families, nature lovers, walkers

Croyde/Woolacombe/Saunton Sands Devon

You know you've nearly reached Croyde when you start to see people walking along the road with surfboards under their arms. This chocolate-box North Devon village has become synonymous with surfing, and with good reason. The waves are fast and hollow, providing challenging conditions for even the most experienced surfer.

Croyde's compact bay is one of a trio of surf beaches that all offer golden sands and magnificent sunsets. The gentler waves along the 5-kilometre (3-mile) long stretches at Woolacombe and Saunton Sands make them more suitable for families and those learning to surf.

Woolacombe is sandwiched between two National Trust headlands, where the cliffs slope down to child-friendly rock pools. These are a

particular attraction in low tide when it's a long walk to the water on this Blue Flag beach.

If you want to escape the summer crowds at Woolacombe, head to **Putsborough** at the southern end of the bay. It's a lovely spot with a sheltered apron of sand at low tide and a car park just above it. Another quiet and sandy beach is **Rockham Bay**, only accessed by foot from **Mortehoe**, where you can park.

From Woolacombe – or neighbouring Croyde – there's an invigorating walk to the National Trust's **Baggy Point** (www.nationaltrust.org.uk), where you can see rock climbers scaling a wall and fisherman hoping for a bite.

The whitewashed, art deco **Saunton Sands Hotel** (www.saunton sands.com) dominates the northern end of the beach of the same name. This beach is a popular place for sand yachting and windsurfing as well as surfing. It also runs North Devon's best beach café just below. Have a

The golden sands of Woolacombe are popular with families and surfers.

Croyde has become synonymous with surfing.

snack or a three-course meal from the deck of the stylish **Sands Café Bar** (01271 891288) as you watch the sunset over the water.

Just behind Saunton is **Braunton Burrows** (www.northdevon biosphere.org.uk), one of the largest sand dune systems in Britain and designated a UNESCO Biosphere Reserve. Watch out for foxes, rabbits, mink and lizards as well as numerous butterflies as you walk across it.

Braunton is a good starting point to cycle or walk along part of the 289.5-kilometre (180-mile) **Tarka Trail** (www.devon.gov.uk/tarkatrail), following the route taken by Tarka the otter, in the classic novel of the same name by Henry Williamson, who lived in the pretty village of **Georgeham**.

The Victorian resort of **Ilfracombe** is worth a day trip, with its high cliffs and rocky beaches bordered by the sweeping **Exmoor hills**. The revamped ancient harbour is home to local Damien Hirst's much-lauded restaurant and bar, **11 The Quay** (www.11thequay.com).

Families will love the **Tunnels Beaches** (www.tunnelsbeaches.co.uk), Ilfracombe's most popular tourist attraction, established in 1823 when four tunnels were carved through the rocks to reach a sheltered beach with a tidal seawater pool, now the proud owner of a Blue Flag award. There's a great café and lots of rock pools and it's open daily from Easter to October.

A good all-weather attraction is **Ilfracombe Aquarium** (www. ilfracombeaquarium.co.uk), located on The Pier, which focuses on local aquatic life. During the summer, if the sun is shining, cruise along the **Exmoor coast** onboard the last ocean-going paddle steamer in the world, *Waverley*, or the motor cruiser, *Balmoral* (www.waverleyex cursions.co.uk). The trips depart from Ilfracombe Harbour.

Take another journey into the past at the **National Trust Carriage Museum** at **Arlington Court** near Barnstaple (www.national trust.org.uk), where you can ride in a horse-drawn carriage and view the collection, ranging from a grand state chariot to a sombre hearse. There's also a Victorian garden and a 'bat cam', where you can spy on the horseshoe bats roosting in the roof of the house.

RIGHT: 'Wipe out' on Croyde Bay.

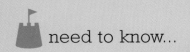

SLEEP Orchard Dene, 2 kilometres (1¼ miles) east of Croyde, is a three-bedroom detached house that sleeps four (one double, two singles). It has an outdoor pool plus a woodburner in the cosy lounge (01326 555555; www.classic.co.uk). **The Little Beach Hotel**, The Esplanade, Woolacombe, is a hip hotel with minimalist rooms overlooking Woolacombe Bay. The hotel is part of Surfed Out's mini-empire, so has own surf school too (01271 870398; www.surfedout.com). **North Morte Farm Caravan & Camping Park**, Mortehoe, is a quiet and well-equipped campsite with a playground and access to a lovely sandy cove at Rockham (01271 870381; www.north mortefarm.co.uk)

EAT Squires Fish Restaurant, Exeter Road, Braunton – celebrity chef Rick Stein loves this award-winning, two-storey fish and chip restaurant with takeaway, which uses local Maris Piper potatoes to make its chips, which are deep-fried in groundnut oil (01271 815533). **11 The Quay**, Ilfracombe, owned by artist Damien Hirst, is the smartest place to eat in the area. There is a bar serving tapas and an upstairs restaurant that offers local Devon beef, excellent fish and great Sunday roasts (01271 868090; www.11thequay.com). **Westbeach Bar & Restaurant**, Beach Road, Woolacombe, is a buzzing bar with modern art and sofas and a rustic-looking restaurant where local crab, lobster and grilled fish dominate the menu (01271 870634; www.westbeachbar.co.uk). **West Hill Farm Shop**, West Down, sells organic produce, including its legendary fresh chocolate sauce (01271 815477; www.westhillfarm.org)

EXPLORE Surf South West, operates in Croyde and Saunton, offers surfing lessons (01271 890400; www.surfsouthwest.com). **Otter Cycle Hire**, The Old Pottery, Station Road, Braunton, hire bikes and are in the perfect spot for you to cycle (or walk) along the Tarka Trail (01271 813339). **Braunton Countryside Centre**, Caen Street Car Park, Braunton, runs nature walks through Braunton Burrows (01271 817171; www.brauntoncountrysidecentre.org.uk)

TOURIST INFORMATION Woolacombe Tourist Information Centre, The Esplanade (01271 870553; www.woolacombetourism.co.uk). **Braunton Tourist Information Centre**, The Bakehouse Centre, Caen Street (01271 816400; www.brauntontic.co.uk). **www.visitnorth devon.com**

GETTING THERE Nearest train station is Barnstaple (17 kilometres (10½ miles) from Croyde). **By road** take the A361 from Barnstaple, then the B3231 to Braunton and follow the signs

GOOD FOR Activity holidays, couples, families, peace and quiet, wildlife enthusiasts

Wembury Devon

It's the wildlife that makes this gently shelving sand and shale beach so special. Seabirds nest in the surrounding cliffs while the wave-cut Blackstone Rocks provide one of the UK's best havens for marine plants and animals in this bay, designated a Voluntary Marine Conservation Area.

RIGHT: Wembury Bay looking towards the Yealm Estuary.

BELOW: The iconic Smeaton's Tower light-house on Plymouth Hoe.

Get there at low tide and you can spot hermit crabs, blennies, sea snails and green sea urchins. One of the best times to see them is in spring, when they have babies and shelter in the rock pools. If you're not sure what you should be looking out for, the **Wembury Marine Centre** (www.wemburymarinecentre.org) on Church Road offers regular rock pool tours from Easter to autumn and it has plenty of interactive displays on local marine life.

After some back-breaking bending over the rock pools, tuck into some home-made cake and tea at the National Trust's **Old Mill Café** (www.nationaltrust.org.uk) at Wembury Beach, a former water-powered corn mill whose old millstones are now used as tables.

You can also visit the imposing **St Werburgh** church, once an important landmark for sailors, perched on the clifftop overlooking the bay.

Wembury isn't the prettiest beach. The sand is greyish and strewn with seaweed but it's incredibly popular, particularly with the locals who arrive for late-afternoon barbecues just as the day-trippers are heading home. When the clifftop National Trust car park is full, people park on the hill leading to the beach, walking through an idyllic flower-filled valley and over a little bridge. The river flows out over the beach and is a good place to make a mini dam or wash your sandy feet.

Look out to sea and you can't miss the **Mew Stone**, a tiny island named after the nesting mews, or gulls, who reside there. In the 1700s it became a prison for a petty criminal who was sentenced to seven years on the island.

A short drive away at **Bigbury on Sea** is **Burgh Island** (www.burghisland.com), home to the art deco hotel immortalized in

Burgh Island is home to an art deco hotel and 14th-century pub – reached by a sea tractor at high tide.

Agatha Christie films, a 14th-century pub and a sandy beach popular with surfers. At high tide, use the bizarre-looking elevated sea tractor on big wheels to reach the island.

Another place worthy of a day trip is **Salcombe**, a pretty nautical town on a picturesque wooded estuary. It has a lush National Trust garden, **Overbeck's** (www.nationaltrust.org.uk), which overlooks the sea.

Wembury is an ideal stop-off for walkers ambling along the **South West Coast Path** (www.southwestcoastpath.com). Head east to **Warren Point** and **Newton Ferrers** on the **Yealm Estuary**, with its bobbing boats, pretty creek-side homes, unspoilt fishing villages and great pubs.

Learn more about the country's maritime heritage by spending a day in **Plymouth**, the departure point for the Pilgrim Fathers, Scott of the Antarctic and US troops during the Normandy Landings. The best sights are on the waterfront such as the **Barbican**, with its narrow cobbled streets and Tudor buildings, craft shops and superb **National Marine Aquarium** (www.national-aquarium.co.uk) where you can see sharks, sea horses and touch some of the fish.

You can't miss the iconic **Smeaton's Tower**, a red and white striped lighthouse. It was once perched on the wave-battered Eddystone Rocks 22.5 kilometres (14 miles) out to sea and was only moved to The Hoe, the grassy clifftop behind the waterfront, when the rock beneath started to crack. Tucked away behind the Quay in the medieval friary is **Plymouth Gin Distillery** (www.plymouthgin.com), where you can see how it is made and learn its history as an official Navy ration. Intoxicating stuff.

RIGHT: Boats on the picturesque Yealm Estuary.

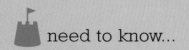

SLEEP Mill Cottage, Wembury Beach, is part of the National Trust-run Old Mill (see page 148). Adjoins the café and beach, with sea views from nearly every room. Sleeps four (0844 8002070; www.nationaltrustcottages.co.uk). **Churchwood Valley**, Wembury Bay, is a collection of secluded timber lodges sleeping up to six in the valley leading to Wembury beach (01752 862382; www.churchwoodvalley.com). **Langdon Court Hotel**, Adams Lane, Down Thomas, is a stylish country-house hotel that was once home to Catherine Parr, the sixth and last wife of Henry VIII (01752 862358; www.langdoncourt.com)

EAT Tanners Restaurant, Prysten House, Finewell Street, serves contemporary British food in Plymouth's oldest building and is where the Pilgrim Fathers ate their last meal (01752 252001; www.tannersrestaurant.com). **The Old Chapel Inn**, near Bigbury on Sea, serves its own smoked meat and fish and honey from their own beehives on their seasonally sensitive menu. Meals are served up in the high-ceilinged Refectory Restaurant (01548 810241; www.oldchapelinn.com). **The Ship Inn**, Noss Mayo, serves light, modern food recommended by Michelin in this cosy, whitewashed creek-side pub (01752 872387; www.nossmayo.com). **Riverford Farm Shop at Kitley**, Yealmpton, has an excellent café using local produce and holds summer barbecues (01752 880925; www.riverfordfarmshop.co.uk)

EXPLORE Wembury Bay Riding School, 83 Church Road, will take you horse riding along the beach. Suitable for beginners (01752 862676). **South West RIB Rides**, rides run from the Barbican, Plymouth, offers fast and bouncy rigid inflatable boat (RIB) rides around Plymouth Sound (01752 777650; www.south-west-rib-rides.co.uk). Walk east along the **South West Coast Path** (www.southwestcoastpath.com) to Warren Point where you can take a **passenger ferry** over the River Yealm to Newton Ferrers and Noss Mayo. Operates daily from April to September (ferryman: Bill Gregor 01752 880079)

TOURIST INFORMATION Modbury Tourist Information Centre, 5 Modbury Court (01548 830159; www.modburytic.org.uk). **www.visitsouthdevon.co.uk**

GETTING THERE Nearest train station is Plymouth (11.5 kilometres (7 miles) from Wembury). **By road** Wembury is signposted off the A379 Kingsbridge to Plymouth road

GOOD FOR Families, walkers, wildlife enthusiasts

Clovelly Devon

Walk down the steep cobbled High Street of this picturesque fishing village in the height of summer and it won't seem like a seaside escape. However, come out of season – or stay the night – and you'll feel like you have the whole place to yourself.

RIGHT: A pretty cobbled lane leading down to the harbour at Clovelly.

Sit on the 14th-century quay and watch the fishermen land their catch while the seagulls wheel above or take a walk along the heavily wooded cliffs, often shrouded in mist, before going to sleep with the sound of the sea thrashing against the shingle.

Day-trippers arriving at **Clovelly** have to leave their cars next to the visitor centre at the top of the hill and pay an entrance fee to access this traffic-free 'museum village', privately owned by the Rous family since 1738. It's worth every penny as it's been preserved much like the National Trust would have done it, with no noisy bars or amusement arcades. The only souvenir shops are in the visitor centre, modelled on a Devon long barn, where you can watch a 20-minute film about the village's history.

The only transport allowed in the village is a Land Rover for hotel guests and their luggage and wooden sledges used by villagers to carry everything from shopping to rubbish. Villagers once used donkeys to transport their goods; horses and carriages couldn't get up the steep streets.

Walk to **The Look-out**, where villagers used to wait and see the fishermen come home. Clovelly was the only safe harbour along this notorious shipwreck stretch of coast between Appledore and Boscastle in Cornwall. Fishing, smuggling and wrecking were the only industries in the 14th century.

Tourism didn't arrive until Victorian times. The village was put on the map by Charles Kingsley, author of *The Water Babies* and *Westward Ho!*. He returned to his childhood home to write the latter, which features Clovelly. Learn more about the man and his work at the **Kingsley Museum** in the village.

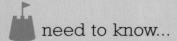

SLEEP Red Lion Hotel, The Quay, has light and airy rooms with sea or harbour views (01237 431237; www.clovelly.co.uk/red_lion_acc.php). **New Inn**, High Street, has William Morris-style rooms, some with sea views, in this olde worlde pub halfway up the High Street (01237 431303; www.clovelly.co.uk/new_inn_intro.php). **55 The Quay** is a bed and breakfast with one double en suite and one twin with private bathroom (01237 431436). **Emily's Cottage**, Buck's Mill, is a self-catering thatched property near Clovelly that sleeps four (01271 813777; www.marsdens.co.uk)

EAT Red Lion Hotel serves Clovelly lobster, game from the estate and vegetables from the gardens – all are used to good effect (see above). **Cottage Tea Rooms**, High Street, is the place for a sandwich or a Devon cream tea. **Quay Shop**, situated in one of the arched cellars of the Red Lion Hotel, sells locally made pasties and other refreshments that you can take away and eat on the harbour. **9 The Quay**, Appledore, is a stylish restaurant in a pink waterfront building serving local specialities such as Clovelly crab thermidor and Taw mussels. Great estuary views (01237 473355; www.9thequay.co.uk)

EXPLORE The Big Sheep, Abbotsham, near Bideford, is an excellent family attraction with self-drive tractors, pony rides, a sheep show and an indoor play area (01237 472366; www.thebigsheep.co.uk). **Skern Lodge**, Appledore, offers a range of adventure activities including climbing, abseiling, assault courses, surfing and kayaking (01237 475992; www.skernlodge.com). **RHS Garden Rosemoor**, Great Torrington, gives you the chance to wander around 30.5 hectares (75 acres) of gardens and woodlands (01805 624067; www.rhs.org.uk/rosemoor). **Broomhill Art Hotel, Sculpture Gardens, Art Gallery and Restaurant**, Muddiford Road, Barnstaple, has 300 or so contemporary sculptures in a 4-hectare (10-acre) garden (01271 850262; www.broomhillart.co.uk/)

TOURIST INFORMATION Clovelly Visitor Centre (01237 431781; www.clovelly.co.uk). **www.visitnorthdevon.com**

GETTING THERE Nearest train station is Barnstaple (33 kilometres (20½ miles) from Clovelly). **By road** Clovelly is on the A39, 16 kilometres (10 miles) west of Bideford

GOOD FOR Activity holidays, couples, families, walkers, wildlife enthusiasts

Marvel at the grapes, peaches and melons growing in the glasshouses at the Victorian walled garden at **Clovelly Court**, home of the Rous family.

Descend the twisting stone **High Street** that drops 122 metres (400 feet) in 800 metres (½ mile), past 16th-century cottages and gardens filled with geraniums and nasturtiums and come out on the tiny 14th-century **harbour**.

From here you can take a boat trip with **Clovelly Charters** (www.clovelly -charters.ukf.net) to Lundy Island onboard *Jessica Hettie*, which is much cheaper and faster than the *MS Oldenburg* from nearby Bideford. *Hettie* can also take you swimming with seals or on deep-sea fishing trips.

Beyond Clovelly there are plenty of other unspoilt villages to explore such as **Appledore**. Situated on the western shore of the mouth of the Torridge, the village has narrow cobbled streets of brightly painted cottages and craft shops. If you crave some sand between your toes head east to the long expanses of golden sands at **Woolacombe** and **Saunton Sands** (see page 144).

If you don't want to drive anywhere there are wonderful walks in both directions from Clovelly along the clifftop. If you head west you pass through dense woodland and along the **South West Coastal Path** (www.southwestcoastpath.com) towards **Hartland Point** lighthouse. You pass the pretty carved folly, **The Angel Wings**, made by a former butler at Clovelly Court, the dramatic headland at **Gallantry Bower** and the natural archways at **Blackchurch Rock** next to **Mouth Mill Cove**, once popular with smugglers.

If you're staying in the village, the **Red Lion Hotel** (www.clovelly.co.uk/ red_lion_acc.php) on The Quay is the best place. Dine on lobster or sea bass landed only metres from your plate before going to sleep in nautically themed bedrooms, lulled by the sound of the sea.

LEFT: High tide at Clovelly's tiny 14th-century harbour.

Clovelly's post office sells postcards and other memorabilia.

Sennen Cove Cornwall

Seals often pop up among the surfers at Sennen Cove, the most westerly beach in mainland Britain. It's also not uncommon to see dolphins frolicking in the waters off this crescent-shaped bay less than 3 kilometres (2 miles) from Land's End.

RIGHT: Sennen Cove, also known as Whitesands Bay, is popular with both surfers and families.

Land's End has a number of tourist attractions.

Sennen's surf is as good as any of the north Cornish coastal resorts and because the waves aren't too steep it's an excellent place to learn. Book a course at the **Smart Surf School** (www.bluelagoonsurf.com), hire boards from the excellent **Chapel Idne Surf Shop** (www.chapelidne.com) or just chill out and enjoy the views from the sleek, glass-fronted **The Beach Restaurant** (www.thebeachrestaurant.com) with its acres of wood and black slate floors. Eat freshly landed lobster from the restaurant's own boat or graze on some home-made bread with tapas as you watch the sunset from the terrace.

Sennen's bleached sand, Blue Flag award and rock pools make it a popular spot for families but it can get packed in the height of summer. If you fancy a bit of tranquillity head north along the beach and scramble over the rocks to neighbouring beach, **Gwenver**.

The harbour area is quite small with a smattering of fishing boats, whitewashed stone cottages, a **Lifeboat Station** (www.sennen-cove.com/lifeboat.htm) and the **Round House and Capstan Gallery** (www.round-house.co.uk), which still has the capstan used to winch boats to shore and displays work from local artists.

When the sea turns rough the sight of the waves breaking over the breakwater can be quite spectacular, with the spray carrying to the top of the **Ped-men-du** headland. From here you can also see **Longships Reef**, scene of countless shipwrecks. You may even spot basking sharks from late spring into summer as you walk towards **Land's End** (www.landsend-landmark.co.uk).

For some, the most south-westerly point in mainland Britain has become too much like a theme park, with its amusement arcades, but

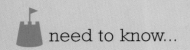

need to know...

SLEEP Old Success Inn is an unpretentious, 17th-century pub with 12 simple but comfortable rooms (01736 871232; www.oldsuccess.com). **Little Cottage** is a thatched semi-detached cottage with beams and a terrace overlooking Whitesand Bay. Sleeps four (01326 555555; www.classic.co.uk). **Whitesands Lodge** provides a range of accommodation – self-catering, tipi camping and a hotel (01736 871776; www.whitesandslodge.co.uk)

EAT The Beach Restaurant serves local, seasonal produce such as Cornish feta salad, catch of the day – from the restaurant's own boat – cassoulet, superb tapas and kids' food served in a contemporary setting with great views (01736 871191; www.thebeachrestaurant.com). **Whitesands Seafood Restaurant and Grill** offers stylish bistro food such as Thai curry, burgers and panini plus local seafood. Barbecues on the decking in summer (01736 871776; www.whitesandslodge.co.uk). **The Gurnard's Head**, near Zennor, serves rich, wholesome fare that's ideal if you've just conquered the South West Coast Path from Sennen (01736 796928; www.gurnardshead.co.uk)

EXPLORE Land's End Riding Centre, Trevescan Farm, offers pony trekking along the cliffs (01736 871989). Take the coast road towards St Ives for one of the most **scenic drives** in the county: gorse and bracken hills, rocky headlands, drystone-walled fields sprinkled with sheep and views of the sea, that's if it's not all shrouded by fog. **Compass West** provides sea-cliff climbing adventures up the granite cliffs of West Penwith. Beginners welcome (01736 871447; www.compasswest.co.uk)

TOURIST INFORMATION Penzance Tourist Information Centre, Station Approach (01736 362207). **www.visit-westcornwall.com**

GETTING THERE Nearest train station is Penzance (14.5 kilometres (9 miles) from Sennen Cove). **By road** take the A30 towards Land's End, approximately 1.5 kilometres (1 mile) before Land's End take the road to Sennen Cove

GOOD FOR Activity holidays, couples, families, wildlife enthusiasts

there are some interesting attractions. **The End to End Story** relates people's journeys from Land's End to John O'Groats and **Air Sea Rescue** is a film following the work of the sea rescuers.

Walkers can avoid the place completely by sticking to the public right of way and focusing on the natural landscape: a mass of incredible rock falls and dramatic cliffs where the might of the Atlantic Ocean meets the Cornish coast. On a stormy day it's an atmospheric place to watch the waves crashing against the rocks. On a clear day you can see all the way to the **Scilly Isles**.

Penzance is the place to go if you want to take a boat over to the unspoilt Scillies but it's also worth visiting for the newly renovated lido and **Penlee House Gallery & Museum** (www.penleehouse.org.uk), Morrab Road, a showcase for many of the artists living in the neighbouring fishing port of **Newlyn**, which has a delightful medieval quay.

Admire sweeping **Mount's Bay** and the iconic **St Michael's Mount** from the National Trust garden **Trengwainton** (www.nationaltrust.org.uk), near Penzance, where enormous tree ferns create a jungly atmosphere.

Other worthy day trips include a visit to **Geevor Tin Mine** (www.geevor.com) in the village of Pendeen, where you can learn about Cornwall's mining industry and take an underground tour. If you like golf, tee off on one of the most spectacularly located courses in the country, **Cape Cornwall** (www.capecornwall.com). You'll have a good excuse for not improving your handicap – the fabulous view.

Dusk at Sennen Cove, the perfect time for a relaxing walk.

LEFT: Trengwainton Garden has an abundance of exotic trees and shrubs.

St Ives Cornwall

You only have to stand on the headland above Porthmeor Beach on a sunny day and see the luminous light bouncing off the Atlantic surf to understand why this former fishing village has became such a haven for artists. It looks like a picture postcard.

The spectacular Porthmeor Beach is popular with families and surfers.

Another testament to the town's artistic legacy, the glazed rotunda of **Tate St Ives** (www.tate.org.uk/stives/), stands proudly on the hillside behind Porthmeor. In fine weather the rooftop terrace is great for an alfresco lunch, the view more than justifying the entrance fee.

Just around the corner below the tiny St Nicholas's chapel, perched on a grass promontory, is the heart of old **St Ives**, with narrow cobbled streets crammed with fishermen's cottages, many of them now home to artists' studios and galleries.

World-renowned sculptor Barbara Hepworth's works are dotted around the town and you can visit the **Barbara Hepworth Museum and Sculpture Garden** (www.tate.org.uk/stives/hepworth/) on Barnoon Hill, where her larger sculptures are framed by lush sub-tropical plants. In the height of summer it provides a tranquil haven from the tourists who parade along cobbled **Fore Street**. It is lined with surf shops, boutiques

OVERLEAF: Walk along the South West Coast Path from St Ives to Gurnard's Head.

The fishing village of Mousehole makes a lovely day trip.

and numerous bakers selling unusual versions of the traditional Cornish pasty and another local speciality, deliciously light saffron buns.

If it's fish and chips you want, head to one of the shops lining the **harbour** where you can watch the world go by. However, keep an eye out for the notorious dive-bombing seagulls trying to steal your dinner.

At low tide there's a lovely walk from the harbour to **Porthminster Beach**, 800 metres (½ mile) of golden sands fringed by palm trees and sub-tropical plants. It's also the end of the line for the charming, late 19th-century **St Erth branch railway** that weaves its way between sand dune and cliff along the coast.

The other, lesser-known town beach is tiny, sheltered **Porthgwidden Cove**, to the north of the harbour, which offers safe bathing and the **Porthgwidden Beach Café** (www.porthgwiddencafe.co.uk).

If it's surf you want there's only one place to go – **Porthmeor**. It is the only town beach facing the mighty Atlantic and has lifeguards, toilets and the **Porthmeor Beach Café** (01736 793366).

If you fancy a change of scene there are plenty of other excellent beaches within an easy drive, including the bleached white sands of **Sennen Cove** (see page 156), **Porthcurno** (see page 166) with the open-air **Minack Theatre** (www.minack.com) perched on the cliffs above and **Lamorna Cove**, a rocky beach at the end of a lush valley where many post-Impressionist artists lived in the early 20th century.

Visit the fortress-like abbey on a tiny island at nearby **St Michael's Mount** (www.stmichaelsmount.co.uk), Marazion, which is only accessible by boat in high tide. There's also the pretty fishing village of **Mousehole** and boat trips to the Scilly Isles from Penzance, which has a revamped lido and numerous art galleries.

One of the nicest ways to appreciate Cornwall's spectacular coastline is to walk along the **South West Coast Path** (www.southwestcoast path.com) from Porthmeor to Zennor, a particularly rugged stretch where you often spot seals and, more rarely, basking sharks. As you reach the headland don't forget to look back and take in the fabulous view.

Right: Surfers riding the waves at Porthmeor Beach, St Ives.

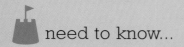

need to know...

ESSENTIAL • INFORMATION

SLEEP Organic Panda B&B and Gallery, 1 Pednolver Terrace, is in a Victorian house overlooking Porthminster Beach. Serves organic breakfasts (01736 793890; www.organicpanda. co.uk). **The Gurnard's Head**, near Zennor, is a lovely gastropub with rooms. Coastal walks on your doorstep (01736 796928; www.gurnards head.co.uk). **Churchtown Farm Caravan & Camping Site**, close to the church, Gwithian, is a quiet, family-run, 2.5-hectare (6-acre) site near Gwithian beach overlooking St Ives Bay (01736 753219; www.churchtownfarm.org.uk)

EAT Porthminster Beach Café has great views and simply cooked fresh fish at London prices. Offers a great-value lunch menu (01736 795352; www.porthminstercafe.co.uk). **Alba Restaurant**, The Wharf, located in the stylish former lifeboat station, specializes in line-caught fish (01736 797222; www.thealbarestaurant.com). **St Andrew's Street Bistro**, 16 St Andrews Street, serves Moro-style food in an eclectic, bohemian interior (01736 797074)

EXPLORE *The Dolly Pentreath* will take you on a trip to Seal Island, a tiny rocky outcrop, where around 100 seals live (01736 797269; www.mlaity. freeserve.co.uk). **St Ives Surf School**, in front of Tate Gallery, on Porthmeor Beach, offers surfing lesssons (01736 793366). **Minack Theatre**, Porthcurno, is a clifftop theatre carved out of the rock with spectacular views (01736 810181; www.minack.com)

TOURIST INFORMATION St Ives Tourist Information Centre, The Guildhall, Street-an-Pol (01736 796297). **www.stives-cornwall.co.uk; www.visit-westcornwall.com**

GETTING THERE Nearest train station is St Ives (London Paddington to Penzance line stops at St Erth, where you can take the branch line to St Ives). **By road** from the A30 take the A3074

GOOD FOR Activity holidays, couples, families, walkers, wildlife enthusiasts

Porthcurno Cornwall

Walk down a lush, narrow valley to this honey-coloured sandy beach hewn
from tiny fragments of broken shells that extend well below the water line,
making the water a shimmering turquoise even on a cloudy day.

*RIGHT: Porthcurno Beach
is an idyllic spot.*

It's not just the beach that makes **Porthcurno** so special. Watching
an open-air performance at the clifftop **Minack Theatre**
(www.minack.com) as the gulls wheel above and the props get knocked
over in the breeze is a particularly memorable experience. Tuck into a
picnic while admiring the views from the 750-seat amphitheatre carved
out of the cliff side. Plays, musicals and operas run from April to
September but the visitor centre is open throughout the year, where you
can learn more about Rowena Cade, the determined lady who built the
theatre in the 1930s.

Look east and you will spot **Logan's Rock**, 66 tonnes (72½ tons) of
granite precariously balanced on **Treryn Dinas** headland, once pushed
on to the beach by a young naval officer in 1824. Huge local outcry led
to the Admiralty forcing him to replace it at his own expense. You can
see the bill and pictures of the restoration at the 400-year-old **Logan
Rock Inn** (www.staustellbrewery.co.uk) in the nearby village of **Treen**.

Another fascinating local attraction is the **Porthcurno Telegraph
Museum** (www.porthcurno.org.uk). Set deep within Second World War
tunnels, behind blast-proof doors, was the biggest telegraph station in
the world. It was first established in 1870 when a cable was laid from
Porthcurno to Carcavellos in Portugal. The whole place was moved
underground at the beginning of the Second World War. Here you can
see how coded messages were sent around the globe through
undersea cable networks.

Walk along the **South West Coast Path** (www.southwestcoast
path.com) towards Penzance and you will come to tiny, unspoilt
Penberth Cove, reached from the main road via a wooded valley
dotted with thatched cottages. Local fishermen still land their catch on

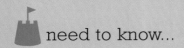

ESSENTIAL • INFORMATION

SLEEP **The Penthouse**, high above Porthcurno beach, is a second-floor, self-catering apartment with stunning views. Sleeps five (01326 555555; www.classic.co.uk). **The Cove**, Lamorna, is a modern apartment hotel at Lamorna Cove, comprising 15 stylish, self-catering apartments, with an outdoor heated pool, sauna, kids' outdoor play area, restaurant, bar and lovely sea views (01736 731411; www.thecovecornwall.com). **Treen Farm Campsite**, 183 metres (200 yards) from Treen Cliffs, St Levan, is a family-run site with two sandy beaches within walking distance and a shop selling the farm's organic milk, yogurt and eggs. Tents and campervans only (01736 810273; www.treenfarmcampsite.co.uk)

EAT **Porthcurno Beach Café**, a few minutes walk from the beach, offers delicious home-made cakes, Cornish pasties and ice cream (01736 810834; www.porthcurno.org.uk). **The Cove**

Restaurant at The Cove, Lamorna (see above), open to non-residents. Newlyn crab and cockle linguine and Cornish beef fillet with handcut chips and béarnaise sauce are served up with the sea views (01736 731411; www.thecovecornwall.com). **Logan Rock Inn**, Treen, specializes in pre-Minack theatre menus and monster steaks and pies. There is a beer garden and coal fires in winter (01736 810495; www.staustellbrewery.co.uk)

EXPLORE **Silver Dolphin Centre**, Trinity House, Wharf Road, Penzance, offers PADI diving courses and guided dives, including night dives from Lamorna Cove, a great place to see sand eels (01736 364860; www.silverdolphinmarine conservationanddiving.co.uk). **Marine Discovery**, Penzance, offers 2½-hour boat trips from Penzance Harbour to the infamous Wolf Rock lighthouse, looking out for pods of dolphins and basking sharks (01736 874907; www.marine discovery.co.uk). **West Cornwall Geology**, run by local Alec Gwynn, will take you on a half-day Land Rover tour to learn more about the geology of the area (07887 556245; www.cornwallgeology.co.uk)

TOURIST INFORMATION **Penzance Tourist Information Centre**, Station Approach (01736 362207). **www.visitwest-cornwall.com**

GETTING THERE **Nearest train station** is Penzance (15.5 kilometres (9.5 miles) from Porthcurno). **By road** from the A30 take the B3315 from Newlyn

GOOD FOR Couples, families, walkers, wildlife enthusiasts

the beach, hauling their boats up the slipway. They may even show you their catch, giving you tips on how to check if fish is very fresh: look at their eyes, they should be transparent. The stream flowing into the sea is excellent for paddling in while the boulder-lined beach is safe for swimming (best at high tide).

Further along the coastal path towards Penzance is **Lamorna** with its small harbour and seaweed-covered granite boulders lining the shore. The beach is reached via a heavily wooded valley, home to many artists. Post-Impressionist artists flocked here in the early 20th century.

Another source of inspiration for local artists is **Mousehole**, the most picturesque fishing village on the **Penwith Peninsula**, with its stone cottages huddled around the harbour and hidden alleyways lined with art galleries and restaurants. It's also famed for its Christmas lights, a spectacular sight as they illuminate the whole harbour, attracting visitors from all over the world.

LEFT: An evening production at the clifftop, open-air Minack Theatre.

Looking east from below the Minack Theatre towards Logan's Rock.

Newquay Cornwall

You may feel slightly out of place if you just sit in a deckchair on the beach in the all-action, surf capital of Britain. Brash and breezy Newquay boasts 10 surf beaches and more surf shops than Bondi Beach.

RIGHT: A surfing contest on Fistral Beach.

BELOW: Newquay's beaches have something to offer everyone.

It's also developing a growing reputation for other adrenalin-fuelled sports such as kiteboarding, kite buggying and the latest craze – stand-up paddle surfing. These activities and more are taught at the Extreme Academy (www.watergatebay.co.uk/extremeacademy.htm) on **Watergate Bay**, to the west of Newquay town centre. Like its sister beach, Fistral,

the 3-kilometre (2-mile) stretch of golden sands at Watergate Bay has had a makeover, with a swish new hotel and equally stylish The Beach Hut café (www.watergatebay.co.uk). Jamie Oliver's Cornwall outpost of Fifteen (www.fifteencornwall.co.uk), also in Watergate Bay, is one of the hottest restaurants in the county, with its Cornish and Italian food, beach views and buzzy atmosphere (breakfast is a good time to get a table).

Fistral remains the king of the beaches, with a fine stretch of golden sand and fast, hollow waves that have bred many professional surfers, an excellent surf school and an equally cool glass-fronted restaurant, **Fistral Blu** (www.fistral-blu.co.uk).

The Eden Project near St Austell is within an hour's drive.

Watergate and Fistral do get very busy in peak season so families might be better off heading to **Crantock**, a small, north-west, sheltered beach and Newquay's best-kept secret. It's the ideal place for little surfers to try out their first waves.

The privately owned sandy beach **Lusty Glaze** (www.lustyglaze.co.uk) is also a good family destination, with lots of activities for restless teenagers. You'll get the shock of your life the first time you see people flying through the air between two cliffs on a zip wire. The beach's **Adventure Centre** (www.adventure-centre.org) also organizes abseiling, rock climbing and coasteering. The latter is an activity where you climb, jump off cliffs and swim – not for the faint-hearted.

There are plenty of family attractions away from the beach geared towards smaller children, such as **Newquay Zoo** (www.newquayzoo. org.uk) and the **Blue Reef Aquarium** (www.bluereefaquarium.co.uk) on **Towan Beach**. **DairyLand** (www.dairyfarmworld. com), just outside Newquay, is a working farm where you can watch cows being milked to music or let the kids run off some steam in the huge undercover play area.

Newquay is the fun capital of Cornwall with many spit-and-sawdust pubs, surf bars and nightclubs to keep you entertained. The town doesn't have much in the way of cultural attractions, but on the cliff north of Towan Beach is the whitewashed 14th-century **Huer's House**, where locals kept watch for approaching pilchard shoals. There's also a lovely hour-long walk along the cliffs to Watergate Bay. Just outside Newquay at Kestle Mill is the National Trust-run Elizabethan manor of **Trerice** (www.nationaltrust.org.uk), with its barrel-roofed Great Chamber, unusual lawnmower museum in the barn and old Cornish apple orchard.

A big all-weather attraction is the **Eden Project** (www.edenproject. com) near St Austell, with its awe-inspiring rainforest and Mediterranean biomes plus a flourishing and vast outdoor garden. Get there late in the afternoon if you want to avoid the worst of the crowds.

If you head north up the coast you can visit **Carnewas and the Bedruthan Steps**, famed for the dramatic views of rock stacks. Owned

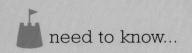

need to know...

SLEEP Headland Hotel, Fistral Beach, is a red-brick, four-star hotel overlooking the beach. The same company also owns self-catering cottages (01637 872211; www.headlandhotel.co.uk). **The House in the Sea**, Newquay Island, is a traditional bed and breakfast on a tiny island overlooking Towan Beach and reached by its own 21.5-metre (70-foot) suspension bridge (01637 881942; www.uniquehomestays.com). **Uluwatu**, 2.5 kilometres (1½ miles) west of Newquay, is a first-floor apartment sleeping five with sea views and only a few minutes' walk from Fistral Beach (01326 555555; www.classic.co.uk)

EAT The Lewinnick Lodge, Pentire Headland, is a stylish restaurant and bar with views over Fistral Beach through its floor to ceiling windows. The food's not bad either: Cornish rib-eye steak, fish cakes and Falmouth bay mussels (01637 878117; www.lewinnick-lodge.info). **Trenance Cottage Tea Rooms**, 2 Trenance Lane, is an oasis from the hustle and bustle of Newquay serving Cornish cheeses, crab and loose-leaf tea in a Georgian cottage (01637 872034; www.trenancecottage tearooms.co.uk). **The Beach Hut**, Watergate Bay, is a stylish café serving up an eclectic menu such as stir-fried squid, Indian curries and Cornish cheese fondue – great comfort food on a windswept day (01637 860877; www.water gatebay.co.uk)

EXPLORE Camel Valley, Nanstallon, produces award-winning wines; sample some during a pre-booked tour (01208 77959; www.camelvalley.com). **British Surfing Association National Surfing Centre**, Fistral Beach, provides surfing lessons (www.nationalsurfingcentre.com; 01637 850737); alternatively you could try **Extreme Academy**, Watergate Bay (01637 860840; (www.water gatebay.co.uk/extremeacademy.htm). **Camel Trail** from Padstow to Bodmin can be explored on foot or on a bike. Part of it runs along a disused railway line traversing the Camel Estuary. Hire bikes through **Padstow Cycle Hire**, South Quay, Padstow, (01841 533533; www.padstowcycle hire.com)

GETTING THERE Nearest train station is Newquay (connections to Par on the London Paddington to Penzance line). **By road** take the A392 off the A30

GOOD FOR Activity holidays, couples, families, walkers

by the National Trust, there's a newly rebuilt cliff staircase down to the beach (closed in winter and not safe for bathing at any time of year; you can also get cut off by the tide). The best direction to walk to appreciate the spectacular coastal views is from Carnewas to Park Head.

If you're craving seafood head to the pretty fishing village of **Padstow** on the Camel Estuary. Splash out on a gastronomic meal at Rick Stein's **Seafood Restaurant** or tuck into fish and chips from his takeaway on the harbour (www.rickstein.com).

Kynance Cove Cornwall

Coastal scenery doesn't get much more wild than Kynance Cove, situated on the wave-battered western edge of the Lizard Peninsula where the cliffs are at their most rugged and the sea is jade green. At high tide you can hear the roaring noise of the blowholes as the waves thrash against the rocks.

RIGHT: The dramatic rock-strewn beach at Kynance Cove.

Another distinctive feature of the coves and beach on the western part of the **Lizard**, an Area of Outstanding Natural Beauty, is the colour of the rock. The best time to see it is when the tide goes out to reveal the almost shiny green skin of the serpentine rock etched with reds and blues. You can buy ornaments hewn from it in stone-turning shops in nearby Lizard Village.

At low tide at National Trust-run **Kynance** (www.nationaltrust.org.uk) you can walk on vast stretches of golden sand and explore the numerous caves and rock pools but beware the strong currents if you want to swim.

You can get a good panorama of the whole cove from the eco-friendly **café** (www.kynancecovecafe.co.uk) with its solar panels and adjoining grass-roofed toilets blending into the landscape. Tuck into home-made cakes, local Cornish pasties, baguettes or that all-important Cornish clotted cream tea.

Walk off all those carbs by heading along dramatic sheer cliffs towards **Mullion**, with its magnificent granite harbour, quaint cobbled slipway, lobster pots and a sandy pocket of beach at low tide. For a more expansive stretch of sand backed by dunes drive to nearby **Poldhu Cove**, which is popular with families.

Away from the beach there's no need to leave the Lizard to enjoy some of the best attractions in the county. The more sheltered eastern edge of the peninsula is the softer side of the Lizard, with the tranquil, wooded **Helford River Estuary** where Daphne du Maurier found inspiration for *Frenchman's Creek*. Buy a gallon of mussels or some fresh Helford oysters from the granite quay at **Porth Navas**, with its exclusive houses, many with their own yacht moorings. At the head of

The village of Cadgwith, where fishing boats still go out every day.

the river is **Gweek**, home to the **National Seal Sanctuary** (www.sea lsanctuary.co.uk), which nurses injured Atlantic grey seals back to health and is open every day of the year except Christmas Day.

Two of Cornwall's best sub-tropical gardens are on the Helford River: **Trebah** (www.trebah-garden.co.uk), a magical ravine garden with giant tree ferns leading down to a private beach on the river; and **Glendurgan** (www.nationaltrust.org.uk), with exotic shrubs, spring displays of magnolias and camellias and a laurel maze for the kids.

South of the Helford River are pretty fishing villages such as **Cadgwith**, the setting for the film *Ladies in Lavender*, which starred Dame Judi Dench and Dame Maggie Smith.

In poor weather, or indeed at any time, children will love **Goonhilly** (www.goonhilly.bt.com), which is situated 11.5 kilometres (7 miles) south of Helston. Once the world's largest satellite earth station with more than 60 dishes pointing to space, it is now home to an interactive Future World exhibition where you can tour Arthur the satellite dish, control a life-size robot, play on an Xbox and run off steam in the indoor and outdoor play areas. It's open every day of the year.

Even people who don't like theme parks will warm to **The Flambards Experience** (www.flambards.co.uk), near Helston, which has all the usual adrenalin-inducing rides plus two excellent educational exhibitions, the Victorian Village and Britain in the Blitz.

You can't go to the Lizard, the southernmost point in Britain, without visiting the distinctive **twin-tower lighthouse** (www.trinityhouse.co.uk), which stands amid the treacherous coast haunted by shipwrecks.

RIGHT: Kynance Cove has numerous caves.

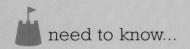

SLEEP **Kynance Cove Cottage**, next to the café, is the place to stay in splendid isolation. It has one bedroom, overlooks the beach, has a woodburner, no TV, phone or mobile reception. Sleeps two (+one/two children) (01326 290436; www.kynance covecottage.co.uk). **Mullion Cove Hotel**, Mullion Cove, has a traditional feel with friendly staff and good food (01326 240328; www.mullion-cove. co.uk). **Trelowarren**, near Mawgan, offers 20 or so eco-friendly self-catering properties on a 405-hectare (1,000-acre) estate with heated pools, tennis court, sauna and hot tubs (01326 221224; www.trelowarren.co.uk)

EAT **The Lizard Pasty Shop**, Beacon Terrace, The Lizard, is a must-visit as you can't come to Cornwall and not try a Cornish pasty; it produces some of the best (01326 290889; www.connexions.co.uk/lizardpasty/). **Roskilly's**, Tregellast Barton, St Keverne, produces delicious organic ice cream and fudge; there is also a restaurant (01326 280479; www.roskillys.co.uk). **The Ship Inn**, Mount Pleasant

Road, Porthleven, is where you can enjoy a drink with a view overlooking the harbour (01326 564204). **Blue Haze**, Mount Pleasant Road, Porthleven, close to The Ship Inn (see above), is a modern, waterfont restaurant that serves dishes such as pan-seared scallops and venison steak. **New Yard Restaurant**, on the Trelowarren estate (see above), offers everything from morning coffee and home-made cake to hand-dived scallops and Falmouth Bay crab risotto for dinner, all sourced within 16 kilometres (10 miles) (01326 221595; www.trelowarren.co.uk)

EXPLORE **Sailaway**, The Boathouse, St Anthony, hires out kayaks, motorboats and sailboats for discovering the Helford River (01326 231357). **Cornish Camels**, Rosuick Organic Farm, St Martin, offers you the opportunity to go camel trekking on the Lizard (01326 231119; www.cornishcamels.com). **Walk it Cornwall**, Lower Halvasso, Penryn, allows you to learn more about the geology, nature and history of the Lizard on a guided day walk (01209 860186; www.walkit cornwall.co.uk)

TOURIST INFORMATION **Helston and Lizard Peninsula Tourist Information Centre**, 79 Menage Street, Helston (01326 565431). **www.visitcornwall.com**

GETTING THERE **Nearest train station** is Camborne (has links with trains to London Paddington; 32 kilometres (20 miles) from Kynance Cove). **By road** take the A394 from Truro to Helston, where you take the A3083 towards the Lizard

GOOD FOR Activity holidays, couples, families, peace and quiet, wildlife enthusiasts

Scilly Isles

The white-sand beaches and unspoilt landscapes of the Scilly Isles have a wild beauty. The archipelago lies 45 kilometres (28 miles) off the coast of Cornwall; tiny pockets of civilization surrounded by the Atlantic and blessed by a mild climate created by the Gulf Stream.

RIGHT: Aerial view of the Scilly Isles.

Just five of the hundreds of islands are inhabited, linked by ferries that run between them as the tides allow. Each island is very different but all have the same sense of peace and feeling of complete escape.

Most people discover **St Mary's** first, arriving by ferry or plane. **Hughtown**, the island's capital, is a bustling place. The high street is lined with sailing lofts and cosy pubs, and sitting on the harbour in the morning gives you the chance to see a very different kind of rush hour; locals and visitors swarming through the streets to catch the inter-island ferries. Inland the island is tranquil and has a mystical feel; rolling heathland dotted with ancient monuments and burial chambers – with 49 kilometres (30 miles) of walks and nature trails to discover.

So close that you can almost walk between them, **Bryher** and **Tresco** are very different islands. Bryher feels wild and untamed, with just one hotel – **Hell Bay** (www.tresco.co.uk/stay/hell-bay) – and a clutch of cottages, edged with deserted beaches that give way to a sea dotted with dramatic rocky outcrops. In comparison, Tresco feels as if it is entirely devoted to tourism. The traffic-free lanes and manicured lawns have a pristine feel that is at odds with the wildness of the other islands.

The best way to discover Tresco is by bike, freewheeling along footpaths that lead into pinewoods or across open land to beaches that you can have all to yourself. Most lanes on the island lead inevitably to the world-famous **Abbey Gardens** (www.tresco.co.uk/see/abbey-garden). The subtropical climate means the gardens have a lush beauty and the range of plants is unparalleled anywhere in the UK. To sit at the top of the gardens, looking down over palm trees and out to the sea beyond, is one of the greatest pleasures the island has to offer.

OVERLEAF: Vast skies above Tresco.

The third biggest island is **St Martin's**, home to some of the most stunning beaches, including **Great Bay**, voted the best beach in the whole of the UK, and **Lawrence's Brow**, where kids will be able to while away hours rock-pooling and picnicking in the dunes that offer shelter from the wind. It's the kind of island where walking doesn't mean waymarked paths and stiles, just gentle rambles over gorse and purple heather.

St Agnes, the fifth and quietest of the islands, offers a similar back-to-basics charm.

One must-see during a stay on the Scillies is the **gig racing**. Every Friday in the summer months crews race the 9-metre (30-foot) rowing boats between the islands. There are boats for spectators to follow the races and cheer on competitors. It's a great way to gain an insight into life on the Scillies but it comes with a warning: the more you feel like a local, the less you'll ever want to leave.

View of Tresco from the island of Bryher.

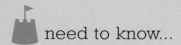

need to know...

SLEEP Hell Bay Hotel, Bryher, combines a feeling of total isolation with luxurious rooms, a fantastic restaurant and has a chic, island-retreat feel (01720 422497; (www.tresco.co.uk/stay/hell-bay). **Gatehouse Cottage**, St Mary's, is a beautifully restored house within the garrison walls, sleeping four (01579 346473; www.duchyofcornwallholiday cottages.co.uk). **Troytown Farm**, St Agnes, is the UK's most westerly campsite, with a small shop and good facilities (01720 422360; www.troy town.co.uk)

EAT The New Inn, Tresco, is recommended by CAMRA and the *Michelin Guide* and serves up fresh fish and classic pub dishes and is very welcoming to families (01720 422844, www.tresco.co.uk/ stay/new-inn). **Juliet's Garden Restaurant**, St Mary's, offers lunches, afternoon tea and supper on an outdoor terrace with glorious views (01720 422228; www.julietsgardenrestaurant.co.uk). **Fraggle**

Rock Café, Bryher, serves Cornish beers and mouthwatering crab sandwiches (01720 422222)

EXPLORE Kestrel Shark & Fishing Trips, St Mary's, will take you on a fishing trip, which is a good way to explore the islands (01720 422251). **Wizard**, St Mary's, will take you on a catamaran cruise (01720 423999)

TOURIST INFORMATION
www.simplyscilly.co.uk

GETTING THERE By air Skybus flies from five south-west airports to St Mary's (0845 710 5555; www.islesofscilly-travel.co.uk). **By ferry** *Scillonian III* runs between Penzance and St Mary's (see above for contact details)

GOOD FOR Activity holidays, couples, families

RESOURCES

GREAT BRITAIN

General
www.blueflag.org
  – *Blue Flag programme for beaches/marinas*
www.forestry.gov.uk
  – *Forestry Commission*
www.goodbeachguide.co.uk
www.nationalparks.gov.uk/
www.nationaltrust.org.uk
  – *National Trust for England and Wales*
www.nts.org.uk
  – *National Trust for Scotland*
www.ramblers.org.uk
  – *Ramblers Association*
www.rspb.org.uk
  – *Royal Society for the Protection of Birds*

Accommodation
Cottage agencies
www.classic.co.uk
www.cottages4you.co.uk
www.english-heritage.org.uk/holidaycottages
www.heartofthelakes.co.uk
www.helpfulholidays.com
www.landmarktrust.org.uk
www.nationaltrustcottages.co.uk
www.premiercottages.co.uk
www.ruralretreats.co.uk
www.statelyholidayhomes.co.uk
www.thebigdomain.com
www.thewowhousecompany.com
www.toadhallcottages.co.uk
www.underthethatch.co.uk – *mostly in Wales*
www.uniquescotland.com
www.vivat.org.uk

Camping
www.coolcamping.co.uk

Hotels, inns and pubs
www.i-escape.com
www.mrandmrssmith.com
www.specialplacestostay.co.uk
www.rarebits.co.uk – *Welsh hotels*

Farm stays
www.farmstay.co.uk

Youth hostels
www.yha.org.uk

Transport
www.nationalrail.co.uk
www.theaa.com
www.thetrainline.com

SCOTLAND

General
www.historic-scotland.gov.uk
www.nts.org.uk
  – *National Trust for Scotland*
www.visitscotland.com

Regions

www.ardanmurchan.com
www.golfhighland.com
www.skye.co.uk
www.visiteastlothian.org
www.visitfife.com
www.visithighlands.com
www.visitscottishheartlands.com

ENGLAND

General

www.english-heritage.org.uk
www.enjoyengland.co.uk
www.nationaltrust.org.uk
  – *National Trust for England and Wales*

North

www.discoveryorkshirecoast.com
www.lake-district.gov.uk
  – *Lake District national park*
www.northumberlandnationalpark.org.uk
www.northyorkmoors.org.uk
www.visitlancashire.com
www.visitnorthumberland.com

East Anglia

www.suffolkcoastal.gov.uk/tourism/
www.visiteastofengland.com
www.visitnorfolk.co.uk

South & South-east

www.iknowdorset.co.uk

www.islandbreaks.co.uk – *Isle of Wight*
www.purbeck.dc.gov.uk/purbeck_tourism.asp
www.visitkent.co.uk
www.visitsussex.org
www.westdorset.com

Devon, Cornwall & The Scilly Isles

www.visitcornwall.com
www.visitdevon.co.uk
www.visitnorthdevon.com
www.simplyscilly.co.uk
www.southwestcoastpath.com
www.trenchermans-guide.com
  – *Eating out in the South-west*
www.visitsouthdevon.co.uk
www.visit-westcornwall.com

WALES

General

www.cadw.wales.gov.uk – *Welsh Assembly's*
  historic environment division
www.visitwales.co.uk
www.walesinstyle.com

Regions

www.llynvisitor.co.uk
www.visitcardigan.com
www.visitpembrokeshire.com
www.visitswanseabay.com
www.pcna.org.uk – *Pembrokeshire Coastal Path*

Index

Picture credits